FROM KITCHEN TO CARNEGIE HALL

FROM KITCHEN TO CARNEGIE HALL

Ethel Stark and the Montreal Women's Symphony Orchestra

MARIA NORIEGA RACHWAL

Second Story Press

Library and Archives Canada Cataloguing in Publication

Rachwal, Maria Noriega, 1981-, author
From kitchen to Carnegie Hall : Ethel Stark and the Montreal
Women's Symphony Orchestra / by Maria Noriega Rachwal.

Issued in print and electronic formats.
ISBN 978-1-927583-87-6 (paperback).--ISBN 978-1-927583-88-3 (epub)

1. Montreal Women's Symphony Orchestra. 2. Stark, Ethel. I. Title.

ML28.M6M82 2015   784.208209714'27   C2015-903307-1

C2015-903308-X

Editor: Marianne Ward
Line and Copyeditors: Carolyn Jackson, Shari Rutherford
Designer: Melissa Kaita

Printed and bound in Canada

*Second Story Press gratefully acknowledges the support of the
Ontario Arts Council and the Canada Council for the Arts for our
publishing program. We acknowledge the financial support of the
Government of Canada through the Canada Book Fund.*

Published by
SECOND STORY PRESS
20 Maud Street, Suite 401
Toronto, ON M5V 2M5
www.secondstorypress.ca

To my little darlings,
Dominic, Anna-Maria, and Susanna,
and my husband, Kamil.

CONTENTS

PROLOGUE
The Struggle for Equality

Today men and women perform side by side in symphony orchestras all over the world, but from its conception in the eighteenth century, the symphony orchestra had been an all-male bastion, a trend that persisted through much of the twentieth century. This elitist tradition systematically excluded women from participating in the creation and performance of symphonic music on the public stage. With the exception of the harpist, who sat almost invisibly on the wings of the stage, professional orchestras in North America and Europe would not hire female musicians, and if they did so, it was reluctantly and usually only until a male replacement could be found. The shortage of equal opportunities for female musicians was the same everywhere in the Western world – New York, Philadelphia, Montreal, Berlin, Vienna, London. Orchestras remained "boys' clubs" where no women were wanted.

Ironically, women were encouraged to study music in order to enhance their marriageability and their chances of moving up the social ladder. Taking music lessons, along with painting, embroidery, and cooking, was considered a part of the proper education of an accomplished lady of good social standing. But this is as far as women were encouraged to pursue any musical aspirations.

Their music-making was deemed appropriate only in the private sphere, where their fathers, husbands, and relatives could monitor their activities. Women were encouraged to be proficient at their instruments but not so accomplished as to threaten male talent.

With the exception of singers, "careers" for female musicians were limited to teaching music lessons to boys and girls, which was essentially an extension of their motherly duties in the domestic sphere. In the late nineteenth century some colleges in North America began to accept female pianists into their programs. Some of the first women who played in public were pianists who graduated from these institutions. Others were child prodigies whose extraordinary talent propelled them onto the international stage. Teresa Carreño, Marguerite Long, and Maud Powell are but three examples. Still others were the wives, daughters, or sisters of famous musicians, such as Fanny Mendelssohn-Hensel, Clara Wieck Schumann, and Camilla Urso. But these women were the exceptions, not the norm.

Furthermore, prevalent rules of etiquette dictated that only certain musical instruments were acceptable for women – those that enhanced their feminine appearance. Keyboard instruments, the harp, the lute, and the guitar, not only highlighted a woman's dainty hands, but also required her to sit for long periods of time, reinforcing a kind of domestic ideology that bourgeois society promoted: woman as passive, submissive, and socially muted. The idea of women performing on traditionally "male" instruments, like the cello or double bass, was a deep source of controversy. Given North America's prudish conventions at the time, it is not surprising that a player's choice or rejection of an instrument often depended on the sexual metaphors evoked by the instrument itself. The curves of the violin, for example, alluded to the female hourglass figure and when played by a man emphasized the male superiority over the female and woman as the object of man's desire, herself an instrument of pleasure.[1] On the other hand, the violin was a soprano instrument, small in dimensions, and did not involve any facial contortions in its playing. This is why the violin was also considered more suitable for women than other string instruments and partly why the violin was one of the first instruments, besides the piano, to be played publicly by pioneering female musicians such as Urso, Powell, and Ethel Stark. The cello, however, was another matter. The possible "immodest" images suggested by the manner of holding the instrument between the legs were enough to dissuade any "respectable" woman from going near it.[2]

By far the most challenging instruments for women to justify playing were the woodwinds, brass, and percussion. These instruments not only had strong military connotations, thus making them "indecent" and unbecoming for women, but they also required the distortion of facial features. Puffing on a tuba, forcing air through a bassoon, pressing the lips to play a clarinet, or flushing the face in trying to get enough air into a French horn was expected of men but thought highly unflattering to women. In his 1904 article, "Opinions of Some New York Leaders on Women as Orchestral Players," Gustave Kerker, a prominent musical director on Broadway, wrote,

> Nature never intended the fair sex to become cornetists, trombonists, and players of wind instruments. In the first place they are not strong enough to play them as well as men; they lack the lip and lung power to hold notes, which deficiency makes them always play out of tune.... Another point against them is that women cannot possibly play brass instruments and look pretty, and why should they spoil their good looks?[3]

Magazines of the early twentieth century suggested how women could look their best while playing musical instruments, while others encouraged them to keep to traditional instruments for the sake of their good looks. Because the image of proper, graceful femininity declined in direct proportion to the size, harshness, and volume of sound produced by an instrument,[4] a woman playing a violin was more tolerated than a woman playing a double bass, and a female flutist was preferred to a female tuba player. Though in reality, none of them were really accepted, simply tolerated for the temporary novelty they created.

The idea that women could play the orchestral music of the great masters as well as men would have been received with contempt or disbelief. Likewise, black musicians – male or female – were also excluded from the roster of the symphony orchestra because blacks, like women, were considered too irrational (or "feminine") to play this exclusive collection of concert music.

The idea of a female conductor was even more ludicrous; indeed, it seemed almost impossible. Commentators who even entertained the idea considered conducting to be too physically and mentally demanding for most women. There was also the lingering prejudice against women's leadership. In the 1940s, a fourteen-year-old girl asked the editor of a music magazine, a former professor at the renowned Oberlin Conservatory in Ohio, "Why is it that nobody has ever seen or heard of an orchestra leader that is a woman?" The professor replied, "Men don't like to play under a woman conductor...[and] people generally don't have as much faith in a woman conductor as in a man.... Like alcohol and driving, home-making and leading an orchestra do not go together very well, and I myself...feel that this is all right."[5] The question of why women were excluded from symphony orchestras has been debated in many accounts of the history of women in music. There were many reasons for their exclusion, but the underlying theme was one of power and control. At the heart of these biased practices was the fear that allowing women into such a traditionally male institution would also weaken other structures of male privilege.

The hiring of women by symphony orchestras did have its occasional vocal supporters amongst male celebrities, though they often did little to ameliorate the situation. The great Leopold Stokowski, conductor of the mighty Philadelphia Orchestra, cried foul at the exclusion of women from the symphonic stage, but in all his years as conductor, he only hired three women: a cellist and two harpists, in the 1934–35 season.[6] The San Francisco Symphony Orchestra attracted national attention when its conductor, Alfred Hertz, hired the first female string players in 1925.

In general, however, conductors and players in major orchestras vehemently resisted the inclusion of women into their organizations. In 1945, conductor Sir Thomas Beecham said, "I do not like, and never will, the association of men and women in orchestras and other instrumental combinations."[7] A male musician had supposedly told Beecham, "If [a woman] is attractive I can't play with her and if she is not I won't."[8] It wasn't until the Second World War that more than a handful of women were accepted into these organizations, though reluctantly and initially only as temporary replacements for the missing men. After all, the war was an abnormal phenomenon that disrupted many lives, and tragic circumstances called for drastic measures. Conscription depleted city orchestras of their male musicians and necessitated the emergency hiring of new recruits to keep orchestras operating, much in the same way that offices, factories, and even the army suddenly relied on women's labor. However, not everyone was thrilled about these new emergency engagements. In 1942, when maestro Fritz Reiner saw an astonishing eighteen women in the Pittsburgh Symphony Orchestra (by far the largest number of women in any major professional orchestra in American history up to that time) he joked sarcastically that his ensemble should change its name to "Fritz Reiner and his All-Girl Orchestra."

This is the daunting uphill battle that lay ahead for any woman wanting to climb the heights of musical performance during the first half of the twentieth century. This was the restrictive environment that a woman had to crusade against if she wanted to set foot on the stage as an orchestral performer or on the podium as a conductor. Blind stereotypes about the emotional, physical, and intellectual nature of woman excluded her from all meaningful employment. As the century progressed, more and more women waged battles against prejudice, as pioneers of the past fought the war before them. But as violinist and conductor Ethel Stark said to K. Linda Kivi for her book *Canadian Women Making Music,* "It didn't matter how good a woman was, she didn't have a chance.... [N]o matter how well she played, she just...was not accepted."[9]

How is it then, that today there are female brass, woodwind, percussion, and string players, and even conductors, of professional symphony orchestras all over North America? The work of pioneers like Canadians Ethel Stark and Madge Bowen would help smash gender ceilings in the orchestral world and open up a new world of opportunities for female musicians.

CHAPTER ONE
The Making of a Maestra

Boulevard Saint-Laurent, also known as The Main, geographically divides the city of Montreal east from west. For much of the 1900s it was also a symbolic line dividing people – the Protestant English-speaking population to the west, the Catholic French-speaking population to the east, and other diverse immigrant communities in the midst or on the fringes, acting as a kind of buffer. The Main was a thriving commercial artery and home to the vast majority of Montreal's Jewish community. It was at her small home in this neighborhood that a Jewish Canadian girl named Ethel Stark first awoke to the reality of the social inequality and injustice in the world around her, and where she first learned the skills and courage required to tread new paths.

Ethel Gertrude Stark was born in Montreal, Quebec, on August 25, 1910, to Adolph Stark and Laura Haupt, émigrés from Ternopol, Austria. They arrived in Canada on August 9, 1907, with their children – two-year-old Jules and four-year-old Doretta – as part of the "The Great Yiddish Migration" from 1880 to 1940 that saw many European Jews, from Russia, Poland, Romania, Austria, and Germany, immigrate to North America. Some came because political conditions in their countries were growing sour, others because anti-Semitic campaigns were being waged against them, and others simply because they had heard North America was the Promised Land, the great paradise on Earth. While many Jewish families merely stopped in Quebec en route to New York and other American cities, others, like the Starks, chose to remain in Montreal, being drawn by the familiar foods, sights, and sounds of the established Jewish community on The Main.

From the beginning Ethel was conscious of the struggles of the Jewish people throughout the world – not only because her family kept such tales alive, but also because Adolph Stark, a barber by trade and later an insurance agent, became the president of the Canadian-Jewish Immigration Society of Montreal and fought for the rights of Jewish immigrants in Canada. Laura Stark was primarily a homemaker, but she also worked outside of the home, helping female immigrants. The Starks were not deeply religious, but they went to synagogue, they knew the Torah, celebrated Jewish holidays, said the traditional prayers, and wanted their children to learn the culture of their people. They considered themselves good Jewish people as well as good Canadians: They practiced the Jewish code of *tzedakah*, of justice and charity.

At ten years of age, Ethel witnessed firsthand what that really meant. One day, her father received news that a Jewish orphan boy from Russia, fourteen-year-old Shepard Broad, had landed in Montreal and was about to be deported back to Belarus. Shepard had lost both of his parents and had decided to join the massive influx of immigrants to North America, hoping he would find his uncle in New York City. He had boarded a ship to what he mistakenly thought was New York but, instead, landed in Montreal. With no papers for entry, Canadian immigration officials were ready to put this "misfit" who spoke no English back on the ship.

Adolph Stark rescued the boy from deportation and took him into his care. He even offered to adopt the boy as his own son. Young Shepard was amazed at such generosity from a complete stranger. Ethel and her siblings, Doretta and Jules, were also rather taken aback. "We don't even know him," Doretta cautioned. But their father insisted that this was the right course to pursue.

The Stark family took Shepard in and treated him as one of their own until they found his uncle in New York. Adolph gave the boy money for the trip, paid for his ticket, and sent him off after he had made him promise to write often. In due time, Shepard became a very successful lawyer who donated to many worthy causes, such as hospitals and schools. Today, the Shepard Broad Law Center of the Nova Southeastern University in Florida stands as a testament to his accomplishments. He never forgot the generosity of the Starks and kept in touch with them, including Ethel and her sister, for the rest of his life.

Such a lesson in generosity was not an isolated one, and the Stark children absorbed these values. Social justice became a vital lens through which they would interpret the world: they would work for what was right.

In addition to their devotion to social work, the Starks were also a highly musical family. Adolph was an amateur violinist, and Ethel's siblings both played the piano. Ethel began formal violin lessons at the age of nine with violinist Alfred De Sève and later studied with Saul Brant at the McGill Conservatory. Ethel loved studying there, but she didn't feel challenged enough. One winter evening after playing a recital, her accompanist confirmed what she already suspected.

"Ethel, you are a wonderful violinist," the accompanist whispered, "but, you won't get anywhere if you stay here. Apply to a big school south of the border. You need competition to help you grow." Although the suggestion startled her, deep inside Ethel knew that this was what it would come down to: She would have to leave Montreal.

The Stark family lived relatively well, but they had no money to send Ethel to a major American or European school. Unfortunately, music education in Canada was lagging behind that of other western countries. The Starks had come from a country with rich musical traditions, where a musician was respected and admired, even more so than lawyers or doctors. Canada was still a dominion of the British Empire, where musicians were compared to people working in the trades, and the government did little to invest in the development of cultural life.[10] The bleak contrast

Ethel began formal violin lessons at the
age of nine, but soon felt the need for
more challenging training than the McGill
Conservatory could offer her.

between Europe's richness and Canada's small-scale system of music education and performance made it difficult for many European immigrants to adjust to their new country.

When she was fifteen years of age, however, Ethel met the famous violinist, Erica Morini, who suggested the young student play for her father, a world-renowned violinist and teacher from Vienna. After hearing her audition, Oscar Morini felt that he had found a musical prodigy and offered Ethel a scholarship if she would go back with him to study in Vienna. This was the opportunity that Ethel had hoped for, but her parents felt their daughter was too young to be traipsing around the world by herself and declined Morini's most generous offer.

Although the Starks did not allow her to go to Vienna, they were nevertheless progressive in encouraging their daughter to pursue her interests and develop her musical skills, especially at a time when female professional musicians were usually frowned upon. As Ethel's friend Yaela Haertz recalled in 2012, "To see a woman playing on stage, alone or with an orchestra, was almost completely unacceptable." The Starks not only wanted Ethel to succeed, but also took steps to make her dream of becoming a professional solo violinist a reality. They supported the idea of a musical career for their daughter. And whereas girls of the time were deterred from being too accomplished lest they threaten their male counterparts, the Starks wanted their daughter to play as well as her talent and training would allow, regardless of her sex. Indeed, an undercurrent of the ideals of women's suffrage persisted in the Stark household throughout Ethel's adolescent years. Such encouragement would go a long way in shaping her confidence in tackling what seemed like formidable and unconquerable obstacles later in her life.

In 1928, when Ethel was seventeen, her brother read that the Curtis Institute of Music (CIM) in Philadelphia provided merit-based full tuition scholarships to talented students. Jules enthusiastically wrote to officials at the Institute requesting an audition for his sister. The administration, however, cautioned him that only the best talent from around the *world* would be admitted. Jules persisted until finally an audition was granted.

Ethel worked extremely hard during her years at the Curtis Institute, winning the admiration of both her instructors and fellow students.

Ethel, her mother, and Jules left for Philadelphia filled with enthusiasm, but when Ethel saw the big turnout of older competing violinists, she felt she had little hope of winning a spot. She played through her pieces and left rather disappointed and with a sour look on her face. The jurors, however, thought Ethel was extraordinarily gifted and offered her a full-time scholarship, making her the first Canadian woman to be accepted into the Curtis Institute of Music.

Thus began a pattern of firsts that would mark Ethel's life and career. Indeed, her acceptance at Curtis was a major accomplishment. At that time many music schools refused to accept female applicants who were not there to become school or private teachers. Ethel's friend Sonia Slatin related a story about a girl who phoned a music college to ask for an audition and was told that only men were given spots, since they were the breadwinners.

Throughout her life, Ethel remained grateful for the sacrifices her family made in order to make her studies at Curtis a success. The first year, Ethel and her mother rented an apartment on Spruce Street, not far from CIM. Laura cooked and cleaned, and Ethel practiced. The following year, Jules and his wife, Annette, moved to Upper Darby, a suburb of Philadelphia, and Ethel moved in with them, allowing Mrs. Stark to return to Montreal. This constant familial support for her music career persisted throughout the course of Ethel's life.

Ethel's years at the Institute were full of joy and opportunity. This was the competitive environment she had longed for. Her time at Curtis, from 1928 to 1933, was also of utmost importance in establishing connections. Most of the students were from foreign lands or from faraway cities in the US, and quite naturally, they bonded with one another. Every student had potential. The great American composer and conductor Leonard Bernstein was one of Ethel's classmates and friends. Violinist Gian Carlos Menotti, composer Samuel Barber, and Lithuanian pianist Nadia Reinsenberg, who would all become celebrities in the years to come, were also fellow students. The Institute was like a giant museum that exhibited the best up-and-coming musicians from around the world. And of course, Ethel studied with many notable teachers, including violinist Lea Luboshutz, who was herself a pioneering female violinist.

By end of the first school year, Ethel had won the admiration of all her violin professors, who in turn sponsored her summer studies with Madame Luboshutz at a cottage in Carmel-by-the-Sea, California. Madame Luboshutz insisted they rent a cottage named for Aimee Semple MacPherson, the first female evangelist minister, though it wasn't until much later that Ethel understood her teacher's insistence on living in a cottage named after a woman pioneer. Madame Luboshutz considered Ethel one of her best students and showed a special favoritism toward her. In fact, Madame encouraged Ethel to spend the following summers at "The Stone House," her private villa for artists in Rockport, Maine. When Ethel complained that she had difficulties practicing with everyone around, Madame ordered a special studio to be built in the back of the house, overlooking the bay, so that Ethel could have some peace and quiet. Ethel practiced for many long hours each day, but that first summer she was rewarded with occasional breaks, walking on the warm, white sand beach and swimming in the glittering Pacific. The following summers in Maine, boating in yachts, riding in new Model T Fords, and eating succulent dinners made up for the long hours of practice. During these summers of diligent study and fun, Ethel also mingled with celebrities and up-and-coming musicians, including Madame's son, the pianist and aspiring conductor, Boris Goldovsky. Long conversations ensued with these musicians about art, cuisine, and music. Here, Ethel made invaluable connections for her future in music.

♪

When Ethel began her studies at the Curtis Institute of Music at age seventeen, she was still largely unaware of the conventions that dictated how women were to behave in society at large. Unlike many girls of her time, Ethel lived in a home environment imbued with the spirit of equality and grew up believing she could be and could do anything she wanted if she tried. Her working mother had provided an unconventional role model for her daughters. Laura Stark was the president of the Ladies' Immigrant Aid Society, the founder of the Ladies Relief Society, and a tireless social worker for the welfare of women and children. A woman working so actively outside the home may have seemed strange to many people in Canada in the early 1900s, including the more orthodox Jewish community, but Laura believed in the pursuit of justice and charity, and her husband fully supported her efforts. She was, in a sense, a suffragette fighting for her own place – as a Jew and as a woman – in a new country. Ethel absorbed her mother's practical feminism and grew to be an assertive and confident woman. "I inherited Mother's inner pride and would brook no indignity, real or imaged, regardless of the consequences," Ethel wrote in her unpublished memoir.[11]

After watching the charismatic, talented, artistic conductor Fritz Reiner in action with the Curtis Orchestra throughout her first year at CIM, Ethel decided she wanted to enroll in his conducting class. It is remarkable that this young girl thought herself worthy of participating in the all-male conducting class, especially since at this time there were very few female role models for her in the field of conducting. Although women had pursued conducting opportunities since the Renaissance, by the 1920s relatively few had established careers in that field. European pianist Josephine Amann-Weinlich first introduced the idea of "women's orchestras" to American audiences when she conducted the Vienna Lady

Orchestra in New York City in 1871. This American tour by a European "lady orchestra" inspired Caroline B. Nichols in 1888 to found The Fadettes Women's Orchestra of Boston, which she conducted until 1918. The most important female pioneer in the field of conducting was British-born Ethel Leginska (1886–1970). She pursued professional opportunities very aggressively, and in the 1920s she became the first woman to appear regularly as guest conductor with major orchestras in Europe and North America. Failing to win a permanent position with a major orchestra, she established her own women's orchestra in Boston in 1926, which she conducted until 1929. Generally, however, in the early part of the twentieth century women conducting publically were a rarity. It is likely that Ethel Stark had heard of these female conductors, but not likely that she had ever seen one in action.

In 1929, before the first semester of her second year at Curtis began, Ethel approached Maestro Reiner, the head of the conducting program, and asked to audition for the class. Reiner was a celebrated conductor who embodied the image of the "conductor-dictator" and had gained notoriety for being tyrannical – even cruel to his musicians. Not surprisingly, Reiner didn't particularly want women in his class. It was, after all, a class for the future leaders and directors of symphony orchestras, and the membership was 100 percent male. Reiner was there to create and shape the Toscaninis, Furtwanglers, and Stokowskis of the next generation – that is, the male dictators of the symphony orchestra. A conducting class was no place for a woman. Ethel was puzzled by Reiner's negative answer and persisted. Still his answer was no, women should not enroll in a conducting class; leadership and woman were mutually exclusive. Even years later Reiner stated that he firmly believed there was "no future for a female orchestra leader with a male orchestra."[12]

The injustice made Ethel more determined to proceed regardless of Reiner's stance. Undaunted, she showed up for the first conducting class of the new semester – uninvited. This was not the first time Ethel had stood up to her elders. As a schoolgirl, she had habitually stormed out of her classroom when her elementary schoolteacher treated her unfairly. The young girl would climb the stairs to Doretta's class and sit with her until the end of the lesson. After a few incidents, her parents and teachers simply accepted that fiery little Ethel tolerated no injustice, real or perceived. But this was the Curtis Institute of Music, and we can only guess what must have gone through her mind. Did she fear being reprimanded? Could she have been expelled for confronting a professor, especially a male one? Was she not risking her performance career by such an act of disobedience?

Reiner was shocked to see her there, questioned her presence, and asked her to leave, but Ethel would not budge. She sat firmly on her chair, surrounded by an assembly of male students, some of whom must surely have looked at her with admiration for having such nerve, others perhaps puzzled by her insistence, and others likely sneering at her as if to say, "What are you doing here? Cooking classes are held elsewhere." Conducting was an art form for men; it was a serious business. But Ethel remained, determined this was the just and right thing to do. Reiner was amused by her tenacity and agreed to let her stay only because he reasoned that she was at Curtis to prepare for a career as a concert violinist and had no intention of becoming a "woman conductor" in the real world. It is extraordinary to imagine this diminutive eighteen-year-old woman not only standing up to a man who has been referred to as a "tyrant," a "sadist," and a "bastard," but also winning the battle.

And so, Ethel Stark became the first woman to be accepted into the conducting program at the Curtis Institute of Music. Whether she knew it or not, she was slowly but surely paving the way for other women in music.

♫

Ethel worked just as hard developing her conducting skills as she did practicing the violin, and over the years Fritz Reiner grew to admire and respect her sheer talent and unwavering work ethic. One sunny day, he was in a particularly good mood and called Ethel in to his studio to play the Tchaikovsky Violin Concerto for him. After she had played about three pages, he put out his hand and said, "That's enough!" Without saying much else, he sent her off. Ethel didn't know whether to shout or blush. Was her violin performance good or bad? It was so typical of him not to say anything about a performance.

Disheartened, she headed straight for the studio of Madame Luboshutz, who greeted her with a big smile and asked in her thick Russian accent, "Vy do you look so sad?" Ethel slumped on the chair and told her what had happened. Madame listened patiently until the end of the animated rant and then said, "Mr. Reiner just called me and said he vuz very pleased with you and that he is scheduling you for an important concert vith ze orchestra! You see, next year the Curtis Orchestra is giving a special concert over the NBC, to be broadcast coast to coast. You have been chosen as the soloist! This is a big compliment to you!"

Dumbfounded, Ethel almost dropped her violin. Mr. Reiner, who didn't particularly like women alone on the stage, either as soloists or conductors, had chosen her to be the main attraction for the NBC performance. Maybe male musicians could learn to be fair in their treatment of female artists after all. Thanks to Fritz Reiner, Ethel would score another first for women and for Canada.

♫

In addition to all the exceptional musical talent at the Curtis Institute, there was something else on exhibit. In a gold and white antique case, resting on plush green cushions and a cream-colored pedestal, was a magnificent Stradivarius violin nicknamed "the Molitor." It had been made in 1697 by the famous violinmaker and was believed to have been owned originally by Napoleon Bonaparte. In 1804, it had been passed on to one of Napoleon's army generals, Count Gabriel Joseph Molitor. Professor Louis Bailey, a fine, short gentleman with a rather large head, sharp, bright eyes, and a habit of wearing red bow ties, had acquired it for the Institute in the summer of 1929 from a dealer in Paris. It was one of his greatest boasts.

"The exhibit was very dramatic," Ethel wrote in her memoir. "Every time I passed by this rare beauty, I felt like kneeling and saying a prayer."

One wintry day, the students at Curtis were shocked to discover the violin missing from its gold case but not at all surprised when they learned that it was in the possession of that industrious and tenacious violinist from Canada, Ethel Stark. Joseph Hofmann, the director of the Institute, had bestowed on her the honor of playing the violin for her coast-to-coast performance of the Tchaikovsky Concerto with Fritz Reiner and the Curtis Orchestra. With that performance, Ethel Stark became the first Canadian woman to play on a nation-wide American radio broadcast and the first woman to perform under Fritz Reiner's baton.

Montreal took great pride in its native daughter and awarded her the city's highest civic honor: Ethel was inscribed in the "Golden Book" of Montreal, one of only a few women, including Queen Marie of Romania, to hold a decoration reserved for world celebrities. The young Jewish woman from The Main was established as one of the city's brightest stars.

CHAPTER TWO

All Aglow with Feminine Charm

The years of the Great Depression brought all sorts of highs and lows in Ethel's life and career. She started off the 1930s as a young, brash, obstinate girl full of zest for the life of a famous concert artist and ended the decade as a mature, altruistic, strong-willed woman whose wider worldview propelled her convictions into action.

In 1933, Ethel Stark performed her final violin graduation recital at the Curtis Institute of Music. Ethel walked onto the stage in a glittering gold gown purchased for her by her teacher, Madame Luboshutz. In the audience sat Mrs. Fritz Kreisler, wife of the world-renowned violinist. She had heard of this promising young Miss Stark and had traveled from New York to Philadelphia to hear her play. Mrs. Kreisler was so impressed with the performance that she called her husband that very evening. Two days later, Ethel and Madame Luboshutz were on the train, chugging along to New York. Fritz Kreisler had invited Ethel to introduce Prokofiev's Violin Sonata at a private party; he had never heard the piece himself, but he knew that Ethel had learned it. Among the guests at the Kreisler home that night were the great Russian composer Sergei Rachmaninoff, the English cellist Felix Salmond, the director of the Curtis Institute, Josef Hoffmann, and Ethel's conducting teacher, Fritz Reiner. Although Ethel had only a day's notice to prepare the piece, the performance was successful and it remained one of the highlights of her life. Afterwards, Hoffmann said, "Ethel, you are now ready to go out into the world to a professional career in music." The young woman trembled with excitement at the thought.

But of course, this was the start of the Depression. The stock market had collapsed a few years earlier, and as the decade progressed the situation worsened. Unemployment rates soared. There was widespread poverty and little opportunity for economic security. Ethel's brother Jules lost his job in Philadelphia and moved to New York. In Montreal, Adolph and Laura Stark were struggling with their finances and with ailing health.

The Depression also affected the music profession. The declining number of positions for musicians in hotels, restaurants, and theaters, as well as the advent of the talking movies, put many musicians out of work. Ethel had engagements booked with many leading orchestras in North America and Europe, but one by one they were forced to cancel. Fortunately, however, her beloved Montreal did not abandon her, despite the fact she had chosen to stay in Philadelphia. Ethel's rising celebrity status coincided with a burgeoning pride in Canadian culture that would gain strength during the Second World War and culminate in the late 1960s. In the years that followed her graduation from Curtis, Ethel played as a guest violinist with the Montreal Orchestra, the Société des concerts symphoniques de Montréal, the Little Symphonies of Montreal, the Toronto Symphony Orchestra, and in recitals on Radio-Canada, including shortwave transmissions to South and Central America. Her playing dazzled critics. Thomas Archer of the *Montreal Gazette* described her as a musician of remarkable technical fluency "who never allows herself to be caught in the snare of virtuosity."[13] Nonetheless, this patchwork career was exasperating for a musician of Ethel's training and expertise, who instead should have been performing on a full-time basis. She wondered if her career would dissolve even before it had officially begun. Sensing her desperation, Jules sent her a few dollars to buy a train ticket to come to New York and take up residence there.

In 1935 Ethel reluctantly parted with her friends in Philadelphia and left for New York to further her career. New York was an irresistible magnet for musicians – from all genres and from all around the world. A great artistic culture proliferated there during the Great Depression. New York was the place to be. Bursting with ambition, Ethel arrived there only to discover that despite the success of a few solo careers, women were excluded from all meaningful professional music activities. Ironically, while the social unrest and misery of the Great Depression gradually provided women with the opportunity to work outside the home in the general labor force, the music profession kept its doors shut.

Now a young woman of twenty-five, Ethel contrasted the encouragement she had received from her parents with the lack of support experienced by many young women musicians in New York, and for the first time she fully appreciated the role model she had had in her own mother. She now understood that society only considered the playing of musical instruments worthwhile for a woman because it gave her greater prospects for marrying into a wealthy family.

In response to the dismal situation of women in music, several "women's orchestras" – chamber string groups for the most part – had sprung up in New York. Ethel was initially excited to learn of these opportunities and of the women who bravely led them, but soon became discouraged when she realized that most "women's orchestras" were vaudeville ensembles composed of a few violinists that combined light classical music with costume changes, poetry readings, and other antics, such as acrobatics. They were paid poorly, if at all. In fact, rather than being paid, the women in these "lady orchestras" often had to pay membership fees for the privilege of playing music. Though it could be argued that this was better than having no opportunity to train in an orchestra, it reveals the inequality that women had to contend with.

In mid-1930s New York, there were a few "serious" women's orchestras that tried to do away with the frolicking of vaudeville. Violinist Frédérique Petrides, for instance, gathered thirty to forty female string players into the Orchestrette Classique in order to create some practical employment and conducting experience for herself and others. Clarinetist Jeannette Scheerer founded and conducted the Women's Chamber Orchestra of New York in 1937. Pianist and conductor Antonia Brico was one of the few women to guest conduct major orchestras in North America and Europe, but she struggled without success to find a steady and permanent conducting position. Instead, she established the New York Women's Symphony in 1934 with the backing of prominent society women. However, finding women who could play woodwind and brass instruments was difficult, and when Brico announced that the group would include men in the 1938–39 season, the board disapproved of the move, citing the feminine spectacle as the strength of the group.[14] It disbanded soon after. Early female pioneers in New York and around the country encountered much prejudice and criticism from the public and the press. Money was always short. Some critics of women's orchestras wondered why women should be paid since they were only "grandmothers and high school girls."[15] And although there were some job opportunities for women in the major orchestras, mostly for harp players, these were very limited and random. If lucky, these women might earn one-third of the wages earned by men.

Ethel now realized how bleak the situation for women musicians really was and how fortunate she was to have been accepted at the Curtis Institute of Music without much prejudice. But now, alone in New York during the Great Depression, she wondered what kind of permanent work, if any, she would be able to do.

What a relief it was when she discovered that Phil Spitalny's "Hour of Charm" Orchestra had an opening in the violin section. The "Hour of Charm" was an elaborate weekly American radio show produced in front of a live audience on the CBS and later NBC networks from 1934 to 1948. It featured director Phil Spitalny and his Musical Queens – a ladies' music ensemble consisting of a few string players, two pianists, a guitarist, a harpist, and some wind and brass instrumentalists. Arrangements of light classical music, popular songs, folk tunes, and religious hymns were part of a typical half-hour program. Performances incorporated smiling women in glamorous gowns, the stage adorned with flowers, ceilings dressed in starlight, and some kind of theatrical component

to finish the show. Millions of music-loving Americans eagerly tuned in week after week.

Ethel did not feel particularly drawn to the theatrics and novelty of it all, but it looked amusing, and she needed a steady job. This was

Phil Spitalny and his "Hour of Charm" orchestra offered Ethel a steady paying position at a time when work was hard to come by. Ethel (second row, second from right) had to swallow her indignation at the conditions of employment, but found she enjoyed being part of the elaborate radio broadcasts.

one of the few paid professional ensembles in the city that accepted women musicians at the time, even though it showcased them as novelties (and sometimes as sexual objects) and not as the serious and educated professionals they were. Given the Depression, this was a rare opportunity for Ethel to make some money while continuing to play violin recitals in Montreal and the New York area. As for her conducting technique, she would have to work on that privately.

At her audition, Phil Spitalny's reaction was one of amazement.

"I have found a gem! A gem!" he repeated over and over again, and he gave Ethel the job on the spot.

Flattered, the young violinist stroked her hair, beaming from ear to ear. But her bright smile began to dim as she listened to Spitalny's incredulous tale.

He related how he and Evelyn Kaye Klein – the main attraction of the "Hour of Charm" – had spent nearly $20,000 traveling across America by car, by boat, and by train to scout out talented women, but there were so few to be found. They had only come up with twenty-two female musicians. Suppressing her growing indignation, Ethel thanked him for the job and walked out of the room. Unbelievable! What about all the highly talented women looking for jobs in this very city? More than three-quarters of the women musicians in New York were unemployed. Ethel soon found out that Spitalny had some very specific requirements for a "female musician." A woman not only had to play *and* sing well, she also had to be single, Caucasian, and highly attractive. She would have to sign a contract to ensure that her weight would be kept under 120 pounds and vow to not enter into a courtship, unless it was approved by him and the orchestra.

Despite her initial hesitation, over the next twelve months Ethel actually enjoyed jamming with the other orchestra members, touring across America, and crooning over the radio waves. She was grateful for the job and for the opportunity to meet new friends, among whom was the talented pianist Sonia Slatin.

Born the same year as Ethel, Sonia Slatin was one of two pianists featured on the "Hour of Charm." Although she was born in New York, she grew up in a family of Jewish immigrants who spoke only Yiddish. At school, the young girl was often taunted by the children and pestered by the teacher, who did not appreciate her "poor" English pronunciation. Sonia found a refuge in music. During Sonia's final year at the Juilliard School of Music, her friend Evelyn Kaye Klein called her up with an offer to join the "Hour of Charm" Orchestra.

Most women would have jumped with joy at the invitation to play for pay. Women were lucky to even get an opportunity to play in public. Besides, Spitalny was one of a few employers who actually paid decent salaries to his female employees. But Sonia was not at all eager to be part of the feminine spectacle. In a letter to her niece she wrote, "I had no experience playing 'popular' music, and I knew this would not only disrupt my hopes of a concert career but could finish it off as well."

Women who performed in female vaudeville ensembles were often belittled and deplored for exhibiting themselves on the public stage and labeled as "loose women with no morals," even marked with the stigma of the prostitute. A woman who wanted a career as a concert artist playing "high art," or classical, music would do well to avoid such morally precarious connections. But the Depression had left Sonia's family with little financial means – her father's garment business was struggling, and her frail mother was not likely to earn much in a factory or office – and of all her family members, Sonia was the only one with the real possibility of making money. "I certainly could not give up the opportunity to make ten or twenty times the amount earned by the average office, store, or factory worker and thus help the family in our predicament," she explained to her niece.

Sonia auditioned, was accepted, and with the other pianist became part of the "Rochelle and Sonia" piano duo. Sonia, Ethel, Evelyn, Rochelle, and the other members of the orchestra gave radio shows, television performances, and toured the country, playing at "movie palaces" such as the Paramount and Capital theaters, Radio City Music Hall, and in such cities as Minneapolis, Detroit, Boston, Chicago, and Toronto.[16] Back then it was highly unconventional for "respectable" women to travel without a male protector or a female companion. Being part of the "Hour of Charm" was liberating because it allowed the women to tour, perform, and see many parts of North America as legitimate female entertainers.

While this was the experience of a lifetime, it also came at a cost. The show downplayed the impressive résumés of its musicians and merely listed their hobbies in their biographies: painting, baking goodies, and collecting dolls. The more serious musicians among them, who wanted to play classical music and do away with the theatrics and vaudeville elements, found it difficult to look like

Ethel's good friend Sonia Slatin (left) was the "Hour of Charm" pianist and was one half of the featured piano duo Rochelle and Sonia.

identical dressed-up dolls wearing fake wigs week after week. Sonia, in particular, had an additional problem. She was nearsighted and needed glasses, but Spitalny refused to let the "image of charm" be tarnished and would not consent to her wearing glasses on stage. As a result, Sonia had to memorize all her music – not only during live shows, but also during all the tours and performances. On one occasion while on tour, he handed out a new piece of music, disregarding the fact that there was no piano for Sonia to practice on. When the show went on air, the orchestra played from their new scores but Sonia played from memory – she had locked herself up in her hotel room for hours and memorized the entire piece without ever having touched the piano.

Ethel and Sonia's similarity in values and outlook was evident from the beginning. They were both superbly talented Jewish women living in an era where discrimination against women musicians was rampant and where girls were led to believe that "looking pretty" with an instrument was significantly more important than playing the instrument well. It was also an era where anti-Semitism was rising and simply being Jewish was enough to arouse suspicion. In each other, Ethel and Sonia found a deep source of consolation, understanding, and friendship. They would remain friends for the rest of their lives. Yet, despite the harmony brought on by their mutual backgrounds and experiences as women, their personalities were vastly different.

Sonia was timid, reserved, and remained modest despite all the honors bestowed on her throughout her life. Ethel was exuberant, self-assured, hot-tempered, and struggled with the temptation to boast about her accomplishments. Where Sonia lacked confidence, Ethel more than made up for it; and where Ethel lacked prudence, Sonia supplied it. Although Ethel could be extremely stubborn in her ways and usually would not listen to other people's opinions, she would always consult Sonia before undertaking major challenges.

On touring nights when the other "Hour of Charm" ladies would go to sleep, Sonia and Ethel would stay up and talk about their hopes for the future – Sonia's modest aspiration of finishing school and being a collaborative pianist, and Ethel's more ambitious dream of being famous and playing the violin on stages all over the world. For now, all Sonia and Ethel could do was dream.

Tchaikovsky's "1812 Overture," with its famous cannon-fire ending, was a crowd favorite during any "Hour of Charm" performance. And Spitalny, who loved spectacle, always finished the performance of this piece with real booming cannons on both side of the stage. The grand finale inevitably brought the crowd to a tremendous standing ovation and many requests for encores. Despite winces and grunts from the orchestra members, the raucous cannon fire continued to boom every now and again.

One day after twelve months of damage to her ears, Ethel decided she had had enough, walked into Phil Spitalny's office, and resigned.

"Not accepted!" was her boss's answer. Violinists like Ethel were hard to come by.

Ethel thought of putting up a fight, but she was momentarily relieved, for she did not have any solid plans for regular employment even though she was still being hired as a guest soloist with orchestras here and there. Leaving the secure financial and musical environment of the "Hour of Charm" seemed all of a sudden too risky. She really did enjoy playing with the ladies and, of course, the good salary. Ethel reconsidered her decision to terminate her contract and ended up staying with the orchestra for another season.

In addition to the theatrics, the show was also known for featuring "Evelyn and her Magic Violin." Evelyn made an appearance at every show by playing a special cadenza she had composed from bits and pieces of the Brahms Violin Concerto. One day while on tour, Spitalny called Ethel into his room and said, "I want you to take over for Evelyn tonight." Evelyn had fallen ill.

Was he serious? The live show would air in one hour!

"Where is the music?" asked Ethel.

"Oh, I haven't got it written down," he replied. "You'll just have to figure it out."

"No," was Ethel's decisive reply.

But Spitalny pleaded, almost on bended knees. "I'm serious, Ethel," he said. "You're the only one who can do it." What a sight, to see her commanding a somewhat overbearing boss like this!

Within the hour the show started. As the curtains opened, the studio audience watched as soft lights glittered like stars, bouquets of white lilies decorated the stage, and a group of beautiful ladies dressed in radiant white emerged from the darkness. For the following half-hour, these "Musical Queens" played through a series of adventures in jazz, swing, classical, and popular hits. As the show came to an end, the audience impatiently waited for the musical acrobatics of "Evelyn and her Magic Violin." The lights dimmed then brightened, but instead of Evelyn, Ethel stood up in her billowing gown with its multiple layers of crinoline and walked to the middle of the stage as the spotlight shone on her. Sonia and Rochelle gasped from their piano benches. Placing the violin to her chin, Ethel smiled and breezed through the cadenza from the Brahms Concerto. The applause from the audience was deafening. Spitalny couldn't have been prouder. He knew Ethel Stark could do it! The orchestra members raved about how great Ethel had sounded on such a short notice. And yes, she had played the entire cadenza from memory.

Ethel earned the admiration of the other musicians, but after a few months of giving it much thought, she again offered her resignation, now confident that the time had come. She had grown to appreciate Spitalny's work with women and even found his arrangements of music to be very good. She enjoyed playing in this entertainment orchestra, but she had conformed to its cosmetic protocol and rather silly shenanigans for far too long. She had no assurance of financial security upon leaving, but she knew she had to pursue the bigger dreams she felt were being limited by her membership in the "Hour of Charm" Orchestra. "I knew it was the right decision," recalled Ethel. Once she had made up her mind, there was no going back.

CHAPTER THREE

About Face

With the "Hour of Charm" behind her, Ethel was able to give free reign to her desires and ambition. She decided to create some practical conducting experience for herself by establishing a serious women's orchestra. No theatrics, no glamour, no dressing up like dolls, just playing good music. Sonia was a graduate student of the Juilliard School, and she happened to know a group of young female students who had been playing in quartets and quintets for some time. Most of them wanted to expand their repertoire, but they had no one to conduct them. A handful of them played in other women's ensembles in the city but wanted more experience. Sonia suggested to Ethel that they look for female students who would be interested in joining. The young ladies would benefit from the experience of playing in an ensemble, and Ethel would be able to gain some valuable conducting experience. Perhaps, if they became good enough, they might even play recitals and radio broadcasts.

Thus, in 1938, Ethel and Sonia co-founded the New York Women's Chamber Orchestra (NYWCO), later called the Women's Little Symphony of New York, with some of the finest up-and-coming female music students from the various colleges and universities in the New York area. This was the first time Ethel had a group of her own to conduct. Now she officially joined Frédérique Petrides and Jeannette Scheerer as pioneering conductors of "lady orchestras" in New York. The NYWCO started out with nine string players, an oboist (Lois Wann), a flutist (Mildred Hunt), Sonia at the piano, and Ethel as their conductor. As their reputation increased, so did their number, and by the end of the year, they were a group of about twenty-five players, mostly strings with some winds – a large chamber group, but not quite what we would consider an orchestra. The three all-female ensembles in the city shared musicians from time to time, especially the woodwind and brass sections, which were hard to fill. Oboist Lois Wann, for example, appeared with Petrides's Orchestrette Classique. Rather than seeing this as competition, the women saw it as an added opportunity. Since performing opportunities were rare, the more the better.

Ethel's NYWCO was an excellent ensemble that performed several weekly concerts over WEVD (a small Jewish classical music station) and gave a series of live concerts around the city. The orchestra also gave Ethel a chance to fine-tune her conducting skills, which had been acknowledged two years earlier, in 1936, when she became the first woman to conduct the Canadian Broadcasting Corporation (CBC) Radio Orchestra in Montreal. Thanks to the NYWCO, Ethel more firmly established her reputation as one of a few women conductors in the world, along with other pioneers Ethel Leginska and Antonia Brico. She was even invited to guest conduct the New York Civic Orchestra – another rare achievement.

At this point in her life, however, Ethel had her heart set on a solo career as a violinist or conductor of a full orchestra rather than managing a little chamber ensemble of music students. As North America recovered from the Depression, Ethel gained more and more musical engagements. With Sonia by her side, she continued to perform many concerts around New York and the surrounding area. She and Sonia decided to embark on a six-month tour of America, giving violin/piano recitals in major cities. They had a great time, enriched their education, expanded their résumés, and came back to New York to present a series of sonata programs over a period of thirteen weeks on radio WEVD. Between playing solo recitals and conducting her small ensemble of women now and then, Ethel was creating opportunities for greater prestige, independence, and artistic control.

In the spring of 1938, more than 150 female members of Local 802 of the American Federation of Musicians – the umbrella organization for the rights of North American musicians – rallied to demand full employment opportunities. This was one of the biggest protests ever staged by women musicians. They discussed ways to combat discrimination. They strategized on how best to smash old-fashioned taboos against playing instruments like the trombone. Antonia Brico questioned why law, medicine, and economics were open to women, but the music profession – orchestras, radio, opera, theater, recordings, and Vitaphone recordings for film – continued to resist female participation.[17] Mary Drier, the vice-president of the Women's Trade Union, suggested that a curtain be used to hide the identity of the musician auditioning for orchestral positions.[18] Talent, not sex, should be the deciding factor, she stressed. The media were invited to cover the event, resulting in several articles that gave a vivid picture of what talented women with higher education and many credentials had to deal with in the music profession: a lack of employment, harassment, sexism, gender stereotypes, and outright discrimination. Some articles pointed out that many women wanted to play traditionally "male" instruments but were criticized for doing so; other articles drew attention to the fact that women in the general labor force were already doing "man's" work in factories...why not in music? Although the rally itself did not fling open the doors of the music profession to women, it nevertheless inspired a new generation of musicians to seek change in the years to come.

Ethel, who was a member of the union, lived through these events, witnessing the tensions, struggles, and also the occasional triumphs achieved by pioneers. She felt the desire to do something about the situation for women in music, but she knew nothing about politics or activism and didn't particularly want to put a stop to her career as a violinist. Despite the struggles brought on

Ethel, seen here conducting, and Sonia Slatin co-founded the New York Women's Chamber Orchestra in 1938. This was Ethel's first chance to conduct a group of her own.

by the Depression, Ethel had found a rather comfortable niche in New York. She had even fallen in love with an intelligent, kind, and attractive businessman, and their relationship was blossoming. Soon, however, her belief in justice and charity was to be put to the test.

♫

It was the end of the 1930s and news of a possible war was spreading quickly. Hitler's National Socialist party had taken power in Germany in 1933 and had passed a series of laws that restricted Jews from participating in public life. They could not own property or work in public office; Jewish children could not go to schools, or to the parks, or to the movies. In the same year that Ethel and Sonia formed their ensemble in New York, 1938, Kristallnacht took place in Germany and parts of Austria on the night of November 9. Jewish synagogues, hospitals, and schools were ransacked, buildings demolished, and the windows of Jewish stores and homes were smashed. Pianos were thrown from second-story apartments to shatter on the streets below. Many Jews had been killed, and thousands of others were being sent to their deaths in Nazi labor camps.

The Starks had family members living in parts of Germany and Austria and heard the news with escalating uneasiness. As the situation worsened and Germany declared war, Canada and the US became more hostile to Jews and restricted the number of Jewish refugees. The seeds of hatred and anti-Semitism were once again planted, nourished, and cultivated in the minds of peoples around the world. Rather than opening up the doors to those in need, governments shut them, out of fear and intolerance. As the president of the Jewish Immigrant Aid Services of Canada in Montreal, Adolph Stark did all he could to help Jewish families in need.

An old Jewish saying, "The man who saves one life, saves the world," was about to put Ethel to the test. The Stark family notified Ethel that one of their relatives, Herman, had tried to flee the Nazis and had been detained at Ellis Island, New York. Before 1924, Ellis Island had been an immigration depot where all immigrants had to be checked before being admitted into the United States. But with the tightening of American immigration policies, by the late 1930s Ellis Island had become a detention and deportation center for undesirable or unfit "aliens." Herman was to be deported back to Germany. Ethel had three days to free him.

She rushed to Shepard Broad's office. The orphan whom Ethel's father had helped escape from Russia was now a successful lawyer in New York. Together, Shepard and Ethel took the ferry to Ellis Island.

The immigration office was an intimidating center, with guards and an area packed with dismal-looking people awaiting their fates: hope for some, and despair for others. "I was escorted to a large room, bare of furniture, with just one wooden bench," recalled Ethel. "One wall was opened with railing so that the guards who paraded back and forth with rifles and bayonets slung over their shoulders could be in constant watch over [the prisoners]." The cold air and the clinical smell of the room made Ethel shudder. She waited for some time in the dead silence, her discomfort growing, until a click of the door startled her. In came the detainee escorted by guards. The door shut with a bang and Ethel was locked up with the prisoner.

"My heart ached when he was brought in, pale, thin, and pathetically scared," she recalled. The detainee told his tale of persecution with the simplest sincerity. Herman was thirty-five years old and had been a successful furrier in Leipzig. He was married and had a baby boy who had been born shortly after he left. After having narrowly escaped the Nazis he had crossed the Atlantic, passing himself off as a tourist. Hoping he would be granted permission to enter the US and then bring his family safely to America, he had arrived in New York with nothing – no luggage, no clothing, no food – except fifty dollars and a few papers in his pocket.

Ethel's response was one of profound empathy. "I witnessed what it meant to be detained and threatened to be returned to enemies, knowing full well that execution will be your fate," she wrote. "I liked him immediately. I promised that by the next afternoon we would have him released. God knows, I knew not how and felt that only a miracle could save him from being deported."

The next afternoon, Shepard Broad and Ethel Stark were summoned to the judge's chambers at Ellis Island and interrogated. This was the moment that would decide Herman's fate. Ethel was concerned, but optimistic. "I knew the mission must be accomplished without fail," she recalled.

"Tell me, your cousin arrives as a tourist for six weeks with reservations at the Piccadilly Hotel with only fifty dollars in his pockets. That does not make sense to me. Can you explain how this is possible?"

Ethel assured the judge that she had no idea but that she would assume all responsibility for him. Shepard Broad, knowing full well that Ethel had no money for such a commitment, stepped up and offered to pay for the expenses. After all, the Starks had helped him escape from Russia, and he believed that *tzedakah* was a motto to live by. The judge eased up when he saw the resolute face of this courageous young woman before him. After a moment's silence, he released the prisoner. Tears of joy wet their faces as they embraced each other on the boat that crossed the waters toward freedom.

In the months that followed, Broad arranged for Herman to enter the country as a legal immigrant. Herman immediately started working as a furrier and tried to contact his wife in Germany, but to no avail. Once the war had broken out, the Nazis had arrested his wife and child and executed them in the gas chamber. Herman's father, who had missed a boat sailing to Canada, had been captured and suffered the same fate – the fate that surely awaited Herman had he been deported.

As Ethel and the two men boarded the Ellis Island Ferry back to the city, she no doubt felt somewhat ashamed to realize how immature she still was – self-absorbed, seeking fame. Making a name for herself as a musician was immense fun, but was there something more she was called to do in life? Could she use her talent to help others in some way? Her parents had set a shining example, but Ethel was not a social activist; she was a musician. She did not deal with people's basic needs; she played music. Yet, there were injustices in the field of music too. Could Ethel be more adamant about promoting women's rights in the field of music?

As for many young women, the war forced Ethel to confront personal hardships – not only Herman's but her own. Her sweetheart was drafted into the army and sent to fight overseas. Although he was not a musician, he was a music connoisseur who appreciated Ethel's talent and encouraged her many endeavors. At last Ethel had found someone she could spend the rest of her life with, but now, she had to face the serious reality that she might never see him again. The hardships of the Depression, the misery of the war, the near miss of Herman's escape from the Nazis, and now the possibility of losing the love of her life gave Ethel new insight into life. Sonia noticed a gradual change in her friend and was pleased to see Ethel, now almost thirty years old, shedding traces of egoism and pride and maturing both as a woman of conviction and as an artist of determined nature. In turn, Ethel could feel the winds of change coming, but little did she know what was in store for her on her return to Montreal.

CHAPTER FOUR
Irresistible Force Meets Immovable Object

One evening in January 1940, Madge Bowen lounged on the sofa in her home in an affluent area of Montreal. She was listening to a live performance of a violin concerto on CBC Radio. Music lifted her spirits. Her three sons and son-in-law were serving in the army overseas, and her beloved husband Henry, a successful Canadian Pacific Railway (CPR) executive, had been commissioned to use his engineering talents for the war effort. As a result, he was hardly ever home, leaving Madge to manage the estate (which included a summer home in Lac Écho and five cottages) on her own, overseeing the servants and the cook and directing the general affairs of the household.

Now fifty-four, Margaret Eleanor Cross Bowen (Madge) had been raised in Ontario in a devout Anglican family who hardly ever missed a Sunday service. As a young woman, she chose to forgo a college education in order to follow a vocation to marriage. With Henry Blane Bowen, she raised three sons and a daughter, and by 1940 she was the proud grandmother of seven. Following the example of her parents, who had a deep concern for the less fortunate, Madge had embraced philanthropy, which she combined with her love for the arts. She supported several

Madge Bowen and Henry Bowen

women's organizations, including the Imperial Order of the Daughters of the Empire, and was so involved with charitable work at her church that the bishop would often drop by her home to visit. The Bowens were also patrons of several organizations in Montreal, including ballet and opera companies and the Ladies' Morning Musical Club, originally founded to give female members a chance to perform music in a public setting and which now brought talent from all over the world to Montreal. It was here that Madge met and befriended many female musicians as well as other ladies from affluent circles, including the wives of public officials and important businessmen.

Madge's husband Henry was an Englishman who had climbed the ladder at the Canadian Pacific Railway, from humble beginnings as an apprentice in the Angus Shops in Montreal in 1905 to chief of motive power and rolling stock in 1928. During his twenty years as a chief mechanical officer, Henry Bowen – intelligent, resourceful, and hardworking – introduced a diverse array of technological developments and innovations to the CPR. Although these accomplishments brought him much respect and even fame, he believed his marriage to Madge, whom he affectionately called Daisy, to be the greatest success of his life.

Although the Bowens were considered part of the higher social classes, they were not born into money. Henry was from a large family in Derbyshire, England. He moved to Canada as a young man in his twenties and was in Toronto learning his craft when he first met Madge. It was blackfly season and Henry became so ill from their bites that he was bedridden for several days. Madge slowly nursed him back to health. They were married in 1909, and together they slowly moved up the social and economic ladder. Madge would have known sacrifices, raising their four children while her husband traveled, educating himself in his field in order to further his career. It would appear that Madge never forgot what it was like to have to work hard to provide for one's family, and she evidently had great respect for people from various economic and social backgrounds. In later years, the Bowen household had a cook and several servants, one of whom was a black woman from Jamaica who helped care for Madge's grandchildren when they spent time at the house. Madge encouraged her grandchildren to kiss their black nanny goodnight, just as they kissed their own grandmother. At a time when racism colored the social atmosphere, this gesture of respect demanded of her grandchildren – to kiss a lower-class immigrant woman – is remarkable and telling of Madge's regard for others.

Madge married Henry in 1909 after meeting him in Ontario.

Madge Bowen worked hard to maintain her social connections, not out of duty, but because she derived pleasure from spending time with others. Her granddaughter, Ann, recalls that Madge loved to host parties – dinner parties, garden parties, tea parties. Although she was shy and soft-spoken, she could be the life of the party when she was among friends. Henry was of a more serious character and didn't always approve of his wife's endeavors, but he supported her nonetheless. He loved her deeply, and his goal was to make her happy.

The Bowens were inseparable – that is, until the war broke out. "My grandfather was working around the clock with the CPR, designing tanks and turning the Angus Shops from the production of engines into the production of tanks for the war," recalls Ann.

In addition to providing comfort during the difficult war years, Madge's love of music also provided a social and creative outlet. She was learning to play the violin, and she joined three friends from the Ladies' Morning Musical Club – violinist Mrs. Norman Herschorn, violist Mrs. E.N. Parker, and cellist May Fluhmann – in forming a string quartet that brought them together once a week. Playing music helped the women pass the time, brought them companionship, and boosted their morale. Occasionally they invited double bassist Gertrude Probyn – a member of the Société des concerts symphoniques de Montréal – to coach them, but more than anything, it was simply fun to play music, and Madge always looked forward to the get-togethers.

As the weeks went on, however, Madge began to wonder: If playing music did so much for her, wouldn't it also benefit other women, especially during this time of war? What if other women with a love of music united to create a larger group? She brought these thoughts to her friends. The challenge would be to create a space, "a room of one's own," where they could make music with other women. Finally Madge decided that her dream – *their* dream – had to become a reality. But how? Who would lead them in a musical world controlled by men, without expecting much in terms of recognition or remuneration? What they needed was a female leader with fiery willpower, a high level of artistic skill, an unwavering determination – someone willing to accept the rough road ahead in staking out their ground.

On this January evening, when the violin concerto ended and the radio host announced the name of the soloist, Ethel Stark, Madge had a sudden idea. Miss Stark was back in Montreal playing various concert engagements. Madge had seen and heard her perform as a violinist and conductor during the young woman's previous visits to the city. Ethel Stark had a lot of experience working with women in New York, and she was one of the few women conductors in the world. Best of all, she was Canadian. Madge flipped through the pages of the phone book until she located the number. Would Miss Stark be so kind as to meet her tomorrow at the Ritz-Carlton Hotel for tea? She had a very important matter to discuss that concerned women in music.

♫

The next day, tea and biscuits were placed on a small table in the lounge at the Ritz. Madge fidgeted nervously as she waited for Ethel Stark. What would the maestra think of working with amateur musicians? Could Madge convince her to undertake such a venture with no promise of success? Once the two women shook hands, Madge took a deep breath and got straight to the point. There were several female musicians, including some who wanted to be professionals in the field, who were interested in forming a group – a string orchestra much like the one Ethel conducted in New York.

"What these women need is a group to be a part of and someone who can mentor them. You, Miss Stark, would be the ideal woman to conduct such an ensemble, here in your hometown. Not only are you highly qualified, but you surely understand the struggles of women musicians."

Ethel was listening attentively, so Madge continued.

"American women are very fortunate to have all-women chamber groups to be a part of. I think it's time we do the same for our Canadian women. There is so much talent here and so much desire. If someone could gather them together for a common purpose, imagine what we could accomplish. Would you be interested in the possibility of starting an all-women's string chamber ensemble here in Montreal?"

Madge's idea was rather progressive for its time, but what she had not counted on was that Ethel Stark was a woman ahead of her time – a visionary – and that "just another" women's string group would not arouse her interest. She already had a small chamber ensemble of women in New York. Besides, the majority of all-women string groups in the US collapsed once the novelty ceased. Ethel looked into Mrs. Bowen's eyes and gave her an emphatic, "No."

Madge sank back into her seat. Had she heard correctly? She had known it was a risk, but deep in her heart she had really hoped for an opportunity.

Ethel continued. "I'm not interested. Any tink town can get an orchestra of strings together. A city of Montreal's population and undeveloped talent should be ashamed to think of forming a group of string players, then calling it a woman's orchestra.... What's wrong with Canada anyway?"[19]

Madge Bowen was completely taken aback, but before she could utter a word, Ethel's demeanor softened and with a twinkle in her eye she said, "I'm not interested, unless it is a full symphony orchestra with strings, woodwinds, brass, and percussion." There was a moment of silence. Ethel continued, "Now that would be quite the feat and well worth my time. Anyone can start a small string orchestra anywhere. But a full symphony orchestra – that's another matter! Then perhaps I would be interested, because it would be entirely different from anything that is out there. A women's symphony orchestra conducted and managed by women would be something that would make me stay in Montreal."

Ethel explained that a string chamber group would not be that radically beneficial to women. If they were to make a significant and lasting impact in the world of orchestral music, playing small chamber pieces for strings would not suffice. To be taken seriously by their audiences, critics, and society at large, female musicians would have to perform the same "big" musical pieces that men played and at a professional level. After pausing a minute, she said, "It must be a large orchestra, with eighty to one hundred players. Mrs. Bowen, I have in mind a symphony orchestra that would measure up to the highest standards. We could call it the Montreal Women's Symphony Orchestra."

Madge's heart raced as she listened to Ethel's sweeping plan. In a matter of seconds, Ethel Stark had raised her initial dream to another level. Madge had not considered such a colossal idea, which would far exceed her own bold plan. To form a complete symphony orchestra consisting of the full contingent of strings, winds, brass, and percussion? And with eighty to a hundred players? Where would they get the women, or the funds, to even start such an enterprise?

This project would be a remarkable challenge and Ethel could only imagine the difficulties they would encounter, but she knew this was the opportunity for change she had been waiting for, and Madge Bowen was the right person to manage the administrative side of such a venture. Madge was clearly a determined, generous, and altruistic woman and had plenty of social connections to build up such a group. For Ethel, this was the time for courage. But what would Madge think of this new idea?

Madge looked straight into Ethel's eyes. She was not one to back down from a challenge either. She nodded and stepped forward as the co-founder and president of this women's organization.

Both women smiled, as if reading each other's mind. The task of forming an orchestra is a tremendous one. They knew they had their work cut out for them.

Having come to an agreement, Ethel's first question to Madge was: "What instrumentation do you have?" Madge's face fell. "Ten or eleven string players," she said. "And maybe a flute player." That was it. Certainly nowhere near enough to make up a full symphony orchestra. How would they recruit so many musicians, especially in the wind and brass sections?

Initially, Ethel proposed they build an orchestra of women with men to fill in the missing chairs. "After all," she said, "when it comes to music, gender should not make a difference." They could prove how well women and men worked together in making music.

But Madge insisted that the orchestra have 100 percent female membership. "If a mixed orchestra succeeded," she argued, "the victory would be conferred to the male membership. If women are to prove the naysayers wrong, we have to do it as women, on our own." Madge spoke quietly but firmly, looking Ethel straight in the eye. "I'm sure I don't have to remind you, Miss Stark, how difficult it is for women to acquire any work or experience in symphony orchestras – as conductors, as soloists, or in the rank-and-file. You yourself have been the victim of such prejudice, have you not?"

Ethel nodded. She wrote of this first meeting with Madge, "To be frank, I liked [the] honest and direct way that she put the case before me. She was a shy woman but...with an iron will. If she wanted something badly enough she would stop at nothing."

As Ethel listened to Madge's rationale, her admiration grew. Madge Bowen was correct. The orchestra had to be conducted by a woman, made up of women, and managed by women. But how would they recruit female woodwind, brass, and percussion players if they didn't exist? At the time in Montreal – and indeed in many parts of North America – there were women who could play the violin, viola, cello, piano, and organ. But there were no women playing woodwind, brass, and percussion instruments. Indeed, Pearl Rosemarin Aronoff, a future member of the orchestra, recalled, "I remember [a] review implying that women's lips could serve a better purpose than on wind instruments." It seems the vast majority of women wasn't willing to tackle such rampant sexism.

Ethel remained quiet for a long time, and Madge began to fear she had been too bold in insisting on an all-female membership. At last Ethel said, " I have a couple of ideas: I will ask some of the women in my previous chamber orchestra in New York to join us on occasion, and I will also scout female musicians in other American colleges to fill in some of the principal chairs." Ethel was sure that the American women would be pleased with the added opportunity of being leaders in a full orchestra.

"But that is only a handful of players at most," replied Madge.

"As for the other players, Mrs. Bowen, if they don't exist, we'll have to make them!" Ethel exclaimed.

It took Madge a few minutes to absorb the impact of such a grand statement. "But how can we start from scratch?" she asked. "It will take us years to get going! And didn't you say, Miss Stark, that you wanted to build an orchestra that would measure up to the highest standards?"

"This is what we'll do," replied Ethel. "Gather up all the

women you can find: pianists, violinists, organists. No previous experience is necessary, except that a woman should know how to read a little bit of music. Ask the women you know, 'Do you have a sister or a friend who plays the piano a little bit, or sings a little bit? Anyone who can read a little bit of music?' Then, I'll assign them to what instrument I think they should play."

"You're suggesting we open up the orchestra to any woman with a desire to play music, those seeking professional careers as well as those who simply want a chance to play in an orchestra?"

Ethel nodded, and Madge's excitement grew. She wanted very much to see the orchestra improve the lives of women – all women. In theory the Ladies' Morning Musical Club was open to all women, but in practice the club catered to a wealthier English-speaking clientele. "If that's the case, then I think our mission should be to make the orchestra inclusive of all women: French, English, young, old, no matter what their background," said Madge. "We women have to band together, especially during this time of war."

Opening up the orchestra to any woman, of any level of talent and of any social class, was a serious idea to consider, let alone execute. Montreal society was heavily stratified based on class, race, and language. Yet, here was a devout Christian woman of the upper class – who was learning to play the violin at age fifty-four – approaching a young professional musician, a Jewish woman, to be her leader. Madge respected Ethel's superb artistry, and Ethel respected Madge's audacity and social vision. Together, they had raised the stakes yet again, and after considering the enormous significance of Madge's proposal, Ethel nodded. "Cooperation, inclusiveness, and hard work will be the ingredients for our success," she said.

Ethel wrote that from the beginning, "The Montreal Women's Symphony Orchestra…was organized for enthusiastic and talented women musicians of all creeds and races."[20] Musical skill was important and clearly in the foreground; there was no question about it. If this orchestra was to succeed, it had to reach professional quality – and quickly. Otherwise, people could blame their slow progress on the fact that they were women. Whatever they did, they would have to do better than men. This was not a cliché but a reality. The few American women who had made it into symphony orchestras expressed again and again that to apply for and win an orchestral position, they had to be far more skilled than the male competitors, not merely just as good. Thus, the orchestra not only had to please but also impress even the most skeptical critics.

Ethel knew that female musicians needed someone who believed in them, someone who would confirm their potential with conviction and in an environment of solidarity, mutual support, and strength in numbers. What the women did *not* need was someone who pitied their situation and made excuses for their lack of opportunities. She claimed, "As soon as [women] encounter an obstacle they're inclined to blame it on discrimination against them." Clearly Ethel was not implying that women were at fault for the sexist attitudes of symphony orchestra boards – indeed, she later stated, "I started the [all-women's] orchestra because I felt that women were not properly treated by orchestra boards" – but she also felt that if women refused to accept the status quo, the barriers would have to be lifted. She stressed, "As for prejudice against them…it's up to the women themselves to overcome that."[21] The instant women rejected stereotypes with conviction, action would follow. That was the key: The women themselves had to want it so much they would be willing to put up with the sweat and tears. Then, quality musical results would follow.

Now that they had agreed on what the ensemble would be, Ethel and Madge were ready to spread the news. But before Madge could grab her coat and purse, Ethel said: "Oh, and one more thing, Mrs. Bowen. See if you can find the volunteers as soon as possible."

Madge cleared her throat. Not only did she have to find dozens of female rebels, idealists, and volunteers to play orchestral music, she was being asked to do so expeditiously. As she watched Ethel put on her coat, she knew she had found the right woman for the job: overbearing, commanding, somewhat egotistical, but definitely determined.

♪

When word got out that a group of housewives, students, and grandmothers were shaking up the established social order by forming a women's orchestra, many people sneered at the idea. Some of those who had previously lauded the achievements of Ethel Stark, solo violinist, weren't sure they liked the idea of her setting up to conduct a women's orchestra in their city. Handling kitchen ladles and spatulas was better use of a woman's time than waving a baton or puffing on a tuba. Others advised that Montreal had too many music ensembles already and an amateur women's orchestra would not be able to stand up to the competition.[22] Besides, weren't women too emotional to take direction from another woman? Others were opposed for economic reasons. What if this women's orchestra eventually wanted to be paid for its services or be funded by the government? Jobs would be taken away from male breadwinners, and this would certainly shake the very foundations of society. Although several professional male musicians applauded the efforts of this charming group of women, others feared that this orchestra would threaten the small pool of available funding and precious stage time, especially in a city with so many ensembles. Others questioned how so many married women with children would find time to rehearse and attend to their domestic duties. Who would care for the children or cook for the husbands while they practiced, rehearsed, and concertized? The living room was deemed a better place for women to perform than the concert hall. "Keep it in your families," they suggested.

By and large, however, the majority of people ignored them and disregarded the rumors of a musical revolution; they were convinced that this so-called "orchestra" of largely inexperienced players would not amount to anything more than a group of ladies gathering for recreation. Besides, most American women's orchestras before the war had disbanded within a few years of their existence, and a large number of those had had men as their leaders or in their ranks. What chance did these women have, especially since they had no initial funding to back them up, no experience running an orchestral organization, and most of them had never set foot on stage? It was indeed laughable. Many predicted the group's swift downfall.

Two years later, Madge recalled the skepticism shown to them in the founding years:

> When people ask me why I took on the task of participating in the affairs of an effort which was consigned, by the "know it all," to a speedy and honourable demise right at the start, I can only answer by pointing with pride…at what our women's orchestra has done…. Montrealers will remember that the very mention of an "all-woman" symphony orchestra merely brought the comment that it would at least provide something novel for the casual concert-goers and curiosity seeker.[23]

Ethel and Madge were determined to beat the odds; in fact, the initial backlash only encouraged them. Unlike men who are often judged to be competent *until* they prove themselves otherwise, as an orchestra of "amateur ladies," they would automatically be viewed as incompetent *unless* they first proved themselves. They knew they could not demand respect; they would have to earn it. The challenge fascinated Ethel, who loved being able to prove sexism wrong, and she delved into the project with her usual intensity, vigor, and determination. Years later when asked why she had agreed to an endeavor of such gigantic proportions, Ethel answered nonchalantly, "Just to prove that we could do it!" As her press secretary stated, "Miss Stark loved challenges. All challenges." And now the challenge was on.

♪

While Ethel and Madge were not surprised by the doubts of the skeptics, they were pleasantly surprised at what they found among women of Montreal. While for much of the twentieth century girls, as a rule, did not study "manly" instruments like the oboe, clarinet, French horn, or timpani, an investigation into the music scene in Montreal revealed that there were many women who preferred the idea of playing wind, brass, and percussion instruments to strings. Thus far, none of these musicians had found much support from their families. Indeed, in a 1946 interview Ethel reminisced, "Our worst headaches were the winds and brasses. We couldn't find enough women who could play these."[24] However, there was plenty of enthusiasm and desire. "So many women who wished to be in the orchestra were timid about their ability, or they needed more training," Ethel explained in the same interview. Within a few days phones were ringing, and women from all across Montreal volunteered to learn to play whatever instrument Miss Stark assigned to them. "You look like you would be very suitable for the bassoon," Ethel said to one, and to another, "You look to me as if you would be able to play the French horn." In a 2010 interview, Ethel recalled, "I made flute players, I made trombones, trumpets, horns, tubas. This is like building the Empire State Building, maybe more than that."[25] The challenge was indeed formidable, but Ethel and Madge were gratified to learn just how many women were also up for the challenge.

Doretta Stark looked on with admiration as woman after woman willingly took up a "strange" and "manly" instrument. She was very pleased that her younger sister had moved back to Montreal and was determined to help with the orchestra in any way she could. In fact, Doretta had dabbled on the oboe here and there but had never had the chance to perform on it. This would be an ideal opportunity.

Not much is known about the lives of the ordinary women who answered the call to form this groundbreaking orchestra. After all, other than the novelty, what interest would there be among the press in a housewife or a maid learning to play the French horn? Unless they went on to major careers after training with the Montreal Women's Symphony Orchestra, the lives of these pioneers have remained invisible. A few of them had received a music education from top schools in America and Europe, but for the most part they lacked the experience of playing in an orchestra. The majority of the members were regular citizens with little or no musical training or experience but with a desire to learn. Helen Demuth, for example, was a high school teacher, married and with children, who could play the violin a little bit. She had never set foot on the stage, and the idea of it made her both nervous and excited. But how would she teach, prepare meals for her family, care for her children, and still have time to practice with the orchestra? Her husband's dinners would have to be neglected now and again.

Brenda Rubin was a secretary by profession and an amateur pianist. With Miss Stark's encouragement, she thought it would be fun to give the flute a try.

In her spare time, Mrs. Herschorn – the wife of a violin teacher – played the violin in Madge Bowen's quartet, but she loved the French horn and thought it would be a good challenge to play something different.

Ruth Hazen, a teenager, had been taking piano lessons for years, but she found the clarinet most fascinating and preferred to spend her time practicing on the wind instrument.

Katherine Schulls, assistant organist at Christ Church of Montreal, volunteered to play the timpani if someone would teach her how.

Another young student, Esther Litman, had recently acquired a bassoon and jumped at the idea of being part of a larger group. Esther later recalled why she chose bassoon and what kept her going: "Idealism, love of music, the chance to play in a symphony, and, perhaps more than anything else, the faith and encouragement of our conductor."[26]

Antoinette Carta, a young girl who studied the violin with Ethel Stark, thought it was a dream come true to be a part of an orchestra.

Likewise, Margaret Adair – Madge Bowen's daughter, married and with children – just couldn't pass up an opportunity to be a part of a symphony orchestra. She became one of the orchestra's piano and celesta players.

Dora Bacal, an unmarried young woman who worked as a secretary in an office, could play a little bit of piano. When Miss Stark suggested she play the French horn, she beamed from ear to ear. Dora found an old, heavily dented instrument at a pawnshop and spent six dollars trying to fix it. Although the instrument had more value as an antique, Dora didn't seem to mind. The thought

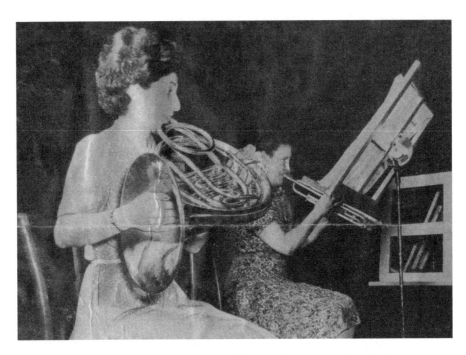

Dora Bacal

of being part of a real orchestra excited her. In the years to come, she would also convince her sisters, Helen and Roselyn, to try the tuba and bassoon, respectively.

Then there was sixty-year-old Marie Brazeau, a French-Canadian seamstress of low income who lived in a rooming house. She was a veteran performer who had once provided behind-the-scenes music for silent film screenings. With the advent of the "talkies," thousands of theater musicians lost their jobs. Marie was one of them. Now she heard with great interest the news of this new orchestra whose mission was to train women in orchestral careers. Marie worked ten hours a day, from eight o'clock to six o'clock – how would she find the time to rehearse? And how would she practice in a rooming house without disturbing the other occupants? Although she was too old for a career as a soloist, the idea of playing music in an orchestra fascinated her. She had not had an opportunity like this when she was younger. Would Ethel Stark consider allowing such an old woman into her organization? Gathering up the courage, she went to the closet and took out her dusty cello.

Some of the new orchestra members – Lyse Vézina, Pearl Rosemarin Aronoff, and Mildred Goodman – had had a taste of the stage and came from musical families. "My father was a musician, knowledgeable, and perhaps the fact there was a woman conducting didn't appeal to him," recalls Pearl, who volunteered to play cello with the orchestra. She had heard about the orchestra from her aunt, Diana Rosemarin, who wanted to play the violin. "My aunt was one of the initial members of the orchestra. She told me about it." The three friends, Pearl, Lyse, and Mildred, were all wonderful string players who had studied music for many years and were craving a chance to play professionally but needed more experience. They formed the core of the string section and served as role models for the beginners.

Young, spontaneous, and highly musical, Lotte Goetzel was a cello student at McGill University trying to gain experience in the world of music. The Goetzels had fled Nazi Germany in 1939 and abandoned their Jewish faith, determined to never again undergo such a traumatic experience. They joined the Unitarian Church and hoped their daughter would follow a career in business and marry a non-Jewish man. But vivacious, adventurous, and determined Lotte had different dreams: She pursued a career in music and later married a Jewish musician, Alexander Brott.[27] Lotte took every opportunity that came her way and when Ethel Stark asked for her assistance, the young woman didn't hesitate to answer in the affirmative.

May Fluhmann, born in 1906 in Roberval, Quebec, was both a cellist and timpanist who had studied at the Juilliard School in New York City until 1929, when her father's illness forced her to return home to Montreal. May was the exception to the general rule of women in symphony orchestras: She was one of three women who played with the English-speaking Montreal Orchestra, from 1937 to 1942, and one of the first women in the world to play timpani professionally. A photo of the Montreal Orchestra from the 1930s shows a female cellist wearing a white blouse – very likely May – juxtaposed against a sea of men with black suits.[28] May had experienced firsthand the struggles that women faced in the world of symphonic music and was very interested in advancing

May Fluhmann

and usually the crowds are about 4,000, with h
turned away at the door for lack of space. 'I
symphony orchestra on this continent cc
entirely of women and conducted by a wor
success.

It is easy to bridge those five years in a few
It was harder to live them and make that
possible.

One of the first needs of the orchestra was a
It was midwinter, and   *Continued on*

Sybil Shattner and Michele Noel,
French horns, Brenda Rubin, flute,
Marie Brazeau, cello

the cause of women. She also played the cello regularly in Madge Bowen's string quartet. When Madge told her that she and Ethel Stark envisioned a top-notch women's orchestra, she volunteered her services and support. She was soon scouting bars, pubs, restaurants, and local coffee shops – any place that might open up leads for female musicians. But first, she approached another woman she knew of, a composer who would not only welcome the opportunity to play in an orchestra, but who was also very much in need of support from other like-minded women.

Twenty-six-year-old Violet Archer sat at the dining table working on her next composition. Born in Montreal on April 24, 1913, to Italian parents, she was raised in Italy until shortly after the First World War. Her family recognized her musical talent and enrolled her in piano lessons at a young age. So determined and enthusiastic was Violet that she never needed any encouragement to practice. But Violet did not want to play the piano just for fun; she wanted to earn a living as a composer. Her father was not pleased. "Music is no profession for a woman," he stressed, pointing to its volatile nature.

Despite the family's opposition, Violet proved to them that she could pay for her own education by accompanying vocal students in the city. When she enrolled at McGill University at the age of seventeen she met even more opposition. Some of her music teachers thought that studying composition was a foolish idea for a woman; one particular teacher thought that Violet's daydreaming would soon "fizzle out."[29] These obstacles only made her more resolved to become a composer.

In 1936, Violet earned her Bachelor's degree in music composition, gained respect for her work despite the controversy she caused by being a female composer, and even had a few paid opportunities for her works. Although she enjoyed composing chamber and choral music, what she really wanted was to compose orchestral music. The sound of the symphony orchestra fascinated her. She attended every concert of the Montreal Orchestra, but she had no experience playing in one.

Tonight she was once again thinking of musical ideas, when she saw a woman with a long winter coat and a thick muff and hat rushing up the walkway. Violet opened the door to May Fluhmann, looking cold but with great excitement glowing in her eyes. Before Violet had the chance to offer her a hot cup of tea, May burst out with her plea.

"Ethel Stark is starting a full-fledged symphony orchestra for women and we need more members. Violet, will you help us?"

As May described the mission of the orchestra, Violet's eyes grew wider and wider. There was just one problem. "I don't play an orchestral instrument," she said.

"That will not be a problem," explained May. "Miss Stark is

Ruth Hazen and Ruth Cowshill, clarinets

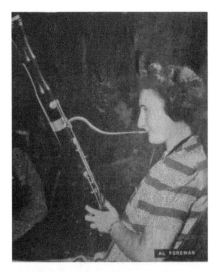

Esther Litman, bassoon;
May Fluhmann, timpani;
Violet Archer, bass drum

recruiting women to learn new instruments. We need a second percussionist. What do you think?"

Violet had never played the percussion before, but May offered to give her a few lessons.

"Rehearsals start next week," May said.

"Next week?"

"Oh yes," continued May. "Miss Stark is not wasting time. We have work to do!"

Violet was thrilled. This was just the opportunity she needed: to be immersed in orchestral sound. Even better, Miss Stark's orchestra offered musical sisterhood.

♫

At last there were enough brave volunteers who would learn wind, brass, and percussion instruments. But there was another large problem: The majority of these women had no instruments on which to learn. New instruments were difficult to find, and even if they were available, who could afford them? Most of the women worked to support their families and had little money to spare. Madge Bowen could not purchase the instruments needed for she would have to invest much of her own funds into jumpstarting the orchestra – placing ads in newspapers to recruit more members and, of course, paying Ethel for her services. Although she couldn't offer Ethel a salary for the countless rehearsals and other duties she would be responsible for, Madge nevertheless felt obliged to offer her payment for each concert. Now here they were, Ethel and Madge, with a shoestring budget, no funding and no sponsors, but plenty of creativity.

First, Ethel rummaged through the city in search of instruments, following leads here and there. People were startled to receive random calls: "I understand your son used to practice clarinet. If you still have it, would you consider selling it to the Montreal Women's Symphony Orchestra?"[30] Over the next few days several used instruments in urgent need of repair were donated. Dents on the bells of trumpets, scratches on the body of flutes, keys that stuck on a clarinet, a reed that wouldn't work on the oboe – all of these would have to be mended somehow. With permission from his uncle Edmond, Rosaire Archambault of Archambault's music store in Montreal agreed to restore some of the older instruments and offered to give the orchestra several used ones. The women were thrilled.

Much to everyone's astonishment, in just ten days the core of the Montreal Women's Symphony Orchestra was complete – a sure sign that the timing of the operation was right. Forty women, armed with forty instruments, had begun their intrusion into one of the last bastions of male supremacy: the symphony orchestra. It wasn't the 80 to 100 women Ethel had envisioned, but she was prepared to begin work with these women.

By forming a full orchestra, one devoid of all the "feminine" trappings of many earlier female ensembles, these women were boldly demanding that they be taken seriously as interpreters of the great works of the classical canon, all written by male composers. Not only that, the broad range of the women's backgrounds would demonstrate that classical music is for everyone, regardless of his or her social standing. The women were essentially expanding the boundaries of the symphony orchestra – a daring thing to do in a highly conservative and somewhat elitist artistic environment like 1940s Montreal. For the next few years, they would navigate their orchestra like a ship at sea, through previously uncharted territory, an unknown course full of perils.

Making up the orchestra was an eclectic group of female suffragettes: young women, older women, students, grandmothers, a seamstress, a photographer's model, a stenographer, several teachers, nurses, office clerks, and some factory workers. According to an early newspaper account, one woman was the head of her household and the other a maid. An older woman was an aunt who played in the orchestra with her niece; they practiced together. There were women who were sisters, as well as a mother and daughter pair. Some women were private music teachers looking for a chance to gain professional training in orchestral playing. Others were housewives participating purely for fun, willing to endure the long hours of practice because they needed an avenue for creative self-expression. There were socialites who lived "uptown" in the prestigious Square Mile – some who needed a creative venue to relieve their boredom – as well as working-class women who lived on The Main – some who would have to make great sacrifices just to find time to practice. There were professional musicians and those with no experience. They were Jewish and Christian, French and English. Their ages ranged from sixteen to sixty. Many of them were considered oddities for having chosen unusual instruments and for thinking they would be able to break into the all-male bastion of the symphony orchestra. But they did not mind being considered so. The thrill of being able to play orchestral music with other women gave them the energy required after a long day of work, whether in the home or elsewhere. Despite their differences, they came together for one purpose: to make music.

CHAPTER FIVE

A Shot in the Arm

The Montreal Women's Symphony Orchestra, the only complete all-woman symphony orchestra in North America at that time – conducted by a woman, managed by women, and composed of women – was born in 1940, the same year that women in Quebec won the right to vote. Perhaps it is no coincidence that these two historic events manifested themselves in the same year. Women were beginning to take their place in the public sphere and gaining the courage to demand equality in the workplace. The wartime shortage of manpower gradually brought about a reliance on "woman power," which in turn generated a sense of pride, independence, and purposefulness in women. They dared to develop themselves politically and artistically, to earn their own livings, and to demand recognition in their chosen fields. Now was the time for these women of Montreal to take their place in shaping public policy with their vote and in expanding the traditional boundaries of the workplace – including the symphony orchestra.

The challenges they faced from the start were many. There was no money to rent a venue large enough for the full ensemble, so for now the orchestra had to be divided into sections based on their instruments. These first sectional rehearsals were held in the kitchens, living rooms, and bedrooms of the women's private homes. Cellist Lyse Vézina vividly remembers moving furniture in her home. "The cellos would be in my kitchen, the violins in the living room, the violas in the bedroom," she recalls. "It was very crammed, but we did it!"

During the initial coaching sessions, each individual section would work on breathing, phrasing, bowing, fingering, and other basics. The more experienced women would help those without any experience. Ethel became a teacher, inspector, and role model. She coached each section privately and moved from kitchen to living room listening to problems and progress. Each woman who had taken on a new instrument was encouraged to take private music lessons.

Ethel lived just off The Main with her mother, father, and Doretta, who was also unmarried and was Ethel's biggest supporter throughout her life. It is rather symbolic that it was in this Jewish neighborhood situated on the dividing line between French and English that some of the initial coaching sessions took place. Here in the Stark home that divisive line with all its ideological under-pinnings was dismantled and replaced by an affirmation of unity, acceptance, and empathy. Ironically, the women would find their efforts to achieve this unity eased by a sense of alienation from the mainstream: Despite winning the vote, they were outsiders, "second-class citizens," and would remain so for many years to come. For Ethel Stark, the challenge was particularly formidable for she was twice marginalized – as a woman and as a Jewish person living in Montreal at a time when anti-Semitic attitudes were prevalent, in a city where Francophones were zealous about preserving their language and cultural identity, and in a country that was controlled by Anglo-Saxon elitists.

From the outset, the Starks were prepared to help the project in any way, big or small. When it was their turn to "host" the orchestra at their home, Ethel's mother would prepare a big jug of lemonade and a large, fresh apple strudel. "My mother was well aware that the majority of the women were by profession teachers, secretaries, and salesladies who worked all day," Ethel recalled. Such was their commitment that "after feeding their own families, they often rushed to rehearsals without grabbing a bite to eat." Further, she said, "weather did not deter them from arriving on time, even in blizzards, snow storms, and fifteen below zero." The food was set on the table at each rehearsal, waiting for the hungry visitors, who quickly devoured the treats.

Within weeks, however, frustration began to set in with what seemed slow progress due to the constant traveling from one area of the city to the next, every other night, week after week. And because there was no large hall, the entire orchestra of approximately forty women had not yet played together. Learning in separate sections was one thing, but playing together as a full orchestra was another. Without practicing as a complete group, progress would continue to be very slow. The MWSO would not be a real orchestra until all the sections were together in one place, playing from one score, and playing simultaneously. But it was the middle of winter and the city's large halls had already been rented out to other groups. Besides, they had no money.

Madge set out to remedy the situation. Finally, after a couple of months of moving from living rooms to bedrooms to kitchens, the landlord of a store on Bishop Street agreed to let them use the basement until it was rented out. Rejoicing at what seemed like a bargain for an orchestra with a scanty budget, the women slogged through four feet of snow to see the new space. Disillusionment followed them down the stairs. The basement was infested with rats, there was no electricity, and there were no chairs. Ever-resourceful, Madge found a great bargain – fifty chairs for ten dollars. But when the chairs arrived, they were in such terrible condition that Madge's husband had to pay an extra forty dollars to repair them.[31]

Despite the setbacks, everyone remained enthusiastic. Now could begin the "real" work of putting together a symphony orchestra. On a cold and wintry night in the dimly lit basement of the empty store on Bishop Street, the women of the Montreal Women's Symphony Orchestra gathered for the first full rehearsal. At last they had found a place where everyone could fit under one roof; at last they had "a room of their own." When Ethel Stark picked up her baton, they all knew that the musical world would never be the same: The Montreal Women's Symphony Orchestra was officially in operation.

As Ethel stood in front of her orchestra for the first time, silence fell over the room. Everyone could feel the excitement, the nervousness, and the energy. Concertmistress Mildred Goodman stood up and signaled the oboist to give the tuning note. One by one each section tuned as best as they could. When the ritual was finished, Mildred sat down and opened up her score. All eyes were now set on Ethel. She raised her baton, and simultaneously, the musicians lifted their instruments into playing position. Ethel took in one large breath and gave a firm upbeat. The orchestra breathed as one and the rehearsal began. A magical resonance, the blaze of a dream being realized, a mystical encounter – these were the things the women expected to experience that first time. But no sooner had the baton come down than squeaks and squawks rang out from the winds and brass. Tuning was off in the strings, and the percussion players soon lost their place in the music. Anyone who has ever tried to learn a new instrument knows that it is no easy task to master the basics. Most professional musicians commence their music education before the age of twelve. Here were secretaries and salesladies who could read "a little bit of music," but were still trying to figure out how to play their instruments.

Playing music – let alone in a public concert – would take months and months of hard work. Ethel had envisioned herself shaping musical phrases, directing subtle changes in harmonies, and indicating dynamic shadings, but instead she found herself like a commander of a ship on the verge of capsizing: beating time, stomping her foot, shaking her head in all directions, making faces when things went wrong, and singing out the missing parts that the novices were not getting. For a moment, the enthusiasm dwindled as reality set in. These were all individuals with a love of music and a desire to see the situation for women in music improve. But could they call themselves an orchestra? Who were they trying to fool?

"It was very difficult. I had to learn how to play in an orchestra," recalled one of the members. "I had to learn to keep one eye on the music and one eye on the conductor. It was not easy. If I looked at Miss Stark, I would soon lose my place in the music."

Although it is impossible to know exactly what went through Ethel's mind that first night, she remained devoted to the project, despite her frustrations. She poured her heart and soul, her enthusiasm and energy, and even her own funds into the orchestra – an orchestra that few believed would amount to much. And if some of the women were disappointed with the initial results, Madge Bowen, on the other hand, was thrilled. She deemed the first rehearsal a great success and redoubled her efforts to find more resources and members. Madge shared Ethel's vision, and this was only the beginning.

In the months that followed, the orchestra members practiced day and night and rehearsed together up to three or four times a week in addition to regular and mandatory sectional work – a schedule almost unheard of in the world of the symphony orchestra.

"That was perhaps the least enjoyable part of the work," recalls Pearl Aronoff. "Ethel would have section rehearsals in her [parents'] home where she would coach the cellos, then the violins, and so on…. We had to climb up those icy stairs." With more than half the women married with children, arranging child care was a major consideration for the players. Putting in so much extra time was a big sacrifice to make, but everyone knew they were starting something remarkable. They were starting a movement of women in music. They were the suffragettes of the symphony orchestra.

Only a few weeks after their first full orchestra rehearsal, misfortune struck. Madge received a phone call from the landlord of the store. He had leased his building, basement included, and the orchestra would have to relocate. Where would they go? They didn't have the funds to rent a big hall, and even if they did, where would they rent one this late in the season? In desperation, the women sought refuge in their churches and former schools. Madge made phone calls here and there. They moved around week after week, again riding the tram, and as Ethel recalls, often in freezing weather to get to their designated rehearsal spaces, which were usually inferior facilities for playing music. The acoustics were terrible, the proper seating arrangement for an orchestra often had to be distorted because of lack of space, and the venues were

Mildred Goodman, Simone Marchand, and Ethel Litman at an early MWSO rehearsal. In the beginning each section of the orchestra rehearsed separately as the women didn't have a space large enough to rehearse together.

often cold. The orchestra was taking a terrible beating – and this was just the beginning. Lugging awkward instrument cases and music stands around from drafty lofts to dimly lit warehouses in the middle of winter was no easy task. But what choice did they have? One night, after one of these rehearsals, Madge made up her mind to use her influence as the wife of Mr. H.B. Bowen, chief of rolling stock at the CPR. She telephoned the president of the CPR, her husband's boss, without consulting Henry first. She pleaded for the use of the lunchroom at the CPR station, explaining how important the orchestra was to women in Montreal, and in North America at large. Could the president lend them a hand?

Within hours, Madge was on her way to collect the night passes required to access the CPR lunchroom in the evenings. The fact that it took Madge almost two weeks to tell her husband what she had done indicates how far out on a limb she had gone on behalf of the orchestra. As a result, the MWSO now had a temporary home. The orchestra members were thrilled. They doubled their practicing efforts in gratitude.

Three months later, at the end of May, Ethel saw how much the women had improved and decided it was time to challenge them yet again. She said to Doretta, "Let's give them a shot in the arm." At the start of the next rehearsal, she announced to everyone, "We'll give our debut public performance in July. Let's get busy!"

A stunned silence blanketed the room.

"Ethel, are you serious?" Madge finally broke the silence. "Could we dare to do such a thing?"

"We need to think about this more carefully," cautioned veteran double bassist Gertrude Probyn. "The orchestra is rather young for a public performance. We also need to consider the opinions of the critics, because if we don't perform well, they could point the finger at our female sex."

"Perhaps we can showcase the string section, or a part of it," added concertmistress Mildred Goodman. "The woodwind and brass players are, for the most part, still learning their instruments. This may not be fair to them. But if we highlight some of our best performers, it could give the public a reason to look forward to our future seasons."

May Fluhmann now pitched in. "Giving a debut performance in July is a rather drastic plan. Mildred's proposal sounds more reasonable."

And the conversation continued, with the women voicing their opinions, offering suggestions, and outright objecting to the proposed plan. But Doretta, who knew her sister all too well, thought it was useless to protest. If Ethel felt this was the right decision, she would listen to no one. She would take such a risk. There was no going back. Ethel was no ordinary woman, and this was no ordinary orchestra.

Ethel tapped the baton and silence fell upon the room once again.

"Let's get busy!" she repeated, and the orchestra members knew they had *a lot* of work to do.

♪

A debut performance for an amateur orchestra was, indeed, a risky venture. The challenge excited Ethel. Besides, she had no doubts that the orchestra could do it. Yet, she would not send the less experienced woodwind and brass players into the battlefield without proper leaders. She called Sonia Slatin, who was still living in New York. Ethel was not in the habit of taking advice from anyone, but she had a special respect for Sonia's prudence and foresight. Sonia had been an important voice in the formation of the orchestra from the beginning, making recommendations and highlighting possible problems.

"I need your help," said Ethel, and told Sonia bluntly that she needed her to find and convince a few key players from the New York area to be a part of the MWSO's debut concert. The beginners should not tackle the frontier alone. "To bolster the group, we need experienced first chair players. We have Lois Wann, the oboist, but we could use two or three others. However, there is no money." Ethel made that last point clear. The orchestra could only pay for their train tickets, and the women could stay either with Madge Bowen or with one of the members of the orchestra.

In fact, Sonia had been expecting this phone call for months. She was particularly excited about being a part of this important Canadian venture. She agreed to help and within a few days she had news to share. "Lois and I have found the players needed for the occasion. They are very pleased and enthusiastic. In fact, their reply was unanimous: 'We would be delighted!'"

♪

The night after Ethel's big announcement, Madge Bowen sat at the dinner table wondering how she would achieve this debut. As the orchestra's president, the bulk of responsibility for handling such a concert, finding sponsors, establishing public relations, launching publicity campaigns, and maintaining important social connections, would all fall on her. She would have to form a board of directors and an auxiliary committee to oversee the planning of the orchestra's activities. She started calling friends and other connections with important positions – anyone who could give the fledgling orchestra a boost, either monetarily or in status. Fortunately, Madge knew the wives of several important Montreal businessmen, public officials, and artists who could be persuaded to lend their names to support this new cultural organization. Having the names of important public figures on the program would give the women's orchestra more credibility.

Madge worked diligently to encourage the support of "society women" – women of the upper class with social and financial means – but she also sought those with a vision for women's rights. One of two founding honorary presidents of the women's orchestra was Thérèse Casgrain, a suffragette and, with Madge, a member of the Ladies' Morning Musical Club. Thérèse Casgrain led the long, hard fought campaign to persuade the Quebec government to grant women the right to vote at the provincial level, a battle finally won in April, three months after the founding of the MWSO. It seems that although Madge Bowen may not have called herself "progressive," she was certainly making it possible for this vision of female empowerment to be realized.

♫

One of the biggest challenges for any performing arts organization is finding rehearsal and performance space. For much of the twentieth century, Montreal was not an ideal city to be in when it came to acquiring first-class venues for music performances. One critic from Toronto even went so far as to claim that Montreal's best auditorium, Plateau Hall, was nothing but a "barn" with terrible acoustics.[32] Nonetheless, Montreal was home to many large orchestras and numerous small chamber groups, and the competition for performing venues was fierce. Weekends were coveted spots for performances. Theaters, libraries, churches, and halls booked early in the season.

If it was difficult for well-funded, established ensembles to find suitable venues, it was twice as difficult for a group of amateur women with no money, used instruments, and whom some people considered a little crazy. Existing ensembles could secure prime rehearsal and performance times by simply "chatting up" their established connections. What chance had a group of amateur female idealists with no previous experience to get into the roster of any respectable venue on a weekend evening three months before their debut concert? Once again, the odds were against them.

Madge and the volunteers from her women's committee scouted venue after venue, but nothing met their budget. They needed free or very affordable space, or a manager who would accept payment at a later date. As the weeks went on Madge began to wonder if the concert would actually materialize or if it was in their best interest to postpone it until the end of the summer when music concert series in the city began to diminish. But Ethel was not the type of person who turned back on promises and refused to hear of canceling the event. One day as Madge was riding the city tram on her way to Ethel's home, she passed by a park and had an idea. Within hours, Ethel, Doretta, and Madge were back on the tram, heading straight for City Hall to ask the mayor for permission to use the chalet atop Mount Royal Park. Within the hour, after many pleas and assurances of how the MWSO was providing a cultural boost to the city of Montreal, permission was granted. There would be a concert on top of the mountain at the end of July.

When the word got out that the women's orchestra of Montreal was actually going to perform a public concert, and in such a short period of time, more incredulity followed. There was one journalist, however, who ignored the gossip and decided to see for himself if these rumors were indeed true. On July 4, 1940, he attended a typical MWSO rehearsal and what he saw caught him by surprise. He wrote with what seems a bit of wonder and awe.

> Just where these 45 or 50 women have come from is a mystery. Certainly the majority have had little or no opportunity to do regular orchestra work before…. [H]ere you have oboists, flautists, clarinet players, tympanists and, be it said, horn players who will maintain their place in view of the public…. There is no question that plenty of hidden talent has been unearthed in the process of forming this orchestra. It is also very obvious that…[they] have been spoiling for a chance such as this one.[33]

He also concluded that Montreal was indeed "due for a surprise" when it discovered that contrary to popular expectations, this was "no amateur group gathered together for the fun of the thing. Nor is it just a passing effort." In fact, he predicted that one day the MWSO could very well rank as number three in its category, behind the Montreal Orchestra and the Société des concerts symphoniques de Montréal.[34] His review provided a much-needed boost for the women's confidence.

Putting together a concert is an enormous task that involves managing many extra-musical projects. There are tickets to print, programs to write, chairs and music stands to reserve, pianos to transport, and most importantly, an audience to gather. Advertising is sometimes as crucial to a performance as rehearsing for one. Simply put, without an audience there is no concert. If there was to be a debut concert on July 31, it had to be publicized. The MWSO was yet again confronted with a financial handicap: There was simply no money for marketing or advertisements. Once again, they would have to be creative and resourceful.

On the morning of the concert, Madge and other women trod the streets, haunted the cafés, and rode the trams of the city, posting little flyers with messages that read, "Debut Concert Tonight, The Montreal Women's Symphony Orchestra, Chalet, Mount Royal Park, 8:45 p.m." Madge thought that if enough people saw the notices in the course of what was predicted to be a very hot day, they would likely want to take in a musical concert on the refreshing mountaintop in the evening. It was a daring approach to take, right at the eleventh hour, but one that also captured the enterprising spirit of the organization: They were not elitists; they were ordinary women vying for a chance to perform. Madge also thought that if a few free tickets were handed out, it would at least assure them some audience in case their tactic failed.

Passing by a group of women distributing tickets by a school that morning was a girl who had recently graduated from high school and was returning home from work. She happily snatched two tickets. "Violet Louise would love it," she thought. She ran to her friend's house to announce the good news.

♫

While the MWSO women were busy preparing for their big debut, another woman was dreaming of making music. Her name was Violet Louise Grant, and her courage, determination, and love of music would propel her a long way.

Little Burgundy was a vibrant area of Montreal situated between Atwater and Guy streets, east and west, and Saint-Antoine to the north. Black immigrants from African countries, the Caribbean, and the American South began settling there in the nineteenth century, living close to the railroad stations and yards of the Canadian Pacific Railway. Black men first came to work on the construction of the railway, aiding Chinese workers. Women sometimes came alone to work as cooks, maids, or housekeepers. Like the Jewish community, the black community kept to themselves and continued to foster their traditions, even though they were small in numbers.

On Saturday nights Little Burgundy would be alive with the sounds of jazz and the sights of dancers on the streets. It was here that Violet's parents, Alfred Nathaniel Grant and Mary Adella Taylor, first met. They were among the first immigrants from Jamaica. After marrying, they saved their pennies to buy a house and raise a family in the neighborhood of Verdun, one of the poorest areas of Montreal. Unlike Little Burgundy, Verdun was a white neighborhood, and for many years the Grants were the only black family in the vicinity.

For many black families, education was much desired but very difficult to attain. Although there were no quotas restricting blacks from attending schools or universities in Montreal, costly prices for books and supplies often prevented low-income students from continuing their attendance at primary and secondary school. Some educators even insisted that it was in "the best interest of the students" to pull black children out of school since they would only become maids, waitresses, porters, shoeshiners, or railroad workers.[35] Prejudice in the form of epithets and racial virulence suffered at the hands of peers, teachers, and administrators also discouraged many black Canadians from continuing

Violet Louise Grant grew up in Verdun and dreamed of making music a career. The MWSO's first performance was also a first for Violet Louise. It was the first time she had ever been to a symphony concert.

their educations. This type of racial intolerance also became a part of the Grants' everyday lives.

Each morning, rain or shine, young Violet Louise and her siblings – Roy, Ivy, and Joyce – would walk to elementary school to the teasing and taunting of a crowd of seven or eight white children, who waited for them at their doorstep.

"Nigger black! Nigger black!"

At the end of the school day, the same entourage of students would gather and escort them back home to the same mocking tunes. Some days, Violet Louise didn't particularly want to go to school. Why did the students sneer at her just because of the color of her skin?

"Keep your head high," her mother would reply.

Although Mr. and Mrs. Grant had not finished high school, they knew a good education was essential to their children's future. They also recognized that the children needed a distraction, a hobby, something to look forward to at the end of the school day, especially after all the cruel bullying.

One afternoon, after a wearisome day at school, Violet Louise and her siblings returned home to a wonderful surprise. Against a far wall in the living room was a beautiful, gently used upright piano. The wear and tear on the piano keys was obvious, but Violet Louise didn't care. She threw her satchel on the floor and dashed to the piano. Days later Violet and her older sister, Ivy, began piano lessons. It was such a thrill to be able to play music. She practiced diligently and dreamed of making music a central part of her life.

This night, on July 31, 1940, she witnessed an event that would change her life forever. Just as Violet Louise was about to sit at the piano and play for her father, there was an urgent knock at the door.

"Violet, you have to come! There is a concert tonight at Mount Royal Park. But, we have to go now. Hurry!"

"What concert?" she asked.

"Miss Stark, the violinist, has an orchestra, and they're playing tonight on top of the mountain! Doesn't that sound like fun?"

Violet looked over to her father. "I would love to go, but we have no money for extravagances. I'm sorry." Violet Louise had never been to a live orchestra concert. There was just no money.

"Don't worry, I have free tickets!"

Violet Louise stopped in her tracks. From the corner of her eye she saw a big grin on her father's face. She grabbed her sweater and ran out the door. A concert on the mountain – it did sound like fun. But they would have to hurry if they wanted to get good seats. As the two friends made their way to the park, Violet Louise's heart raced. This would be her first live concert. What would it be like? What would they play?

♪

That evening, July 31, 1940, the women of the Montreal Women's Symphony Orchestra prepared for their concert debut at the Chalet of Mount Royal Park.

Dora Bacal had been nervous and excited the entire day. Her

debut concert had been the subject of conversation with the other secretaries at the office. At three o'clock she grabbed her purse, rushed out of the office, and made her way to the final dress rehearsal. The rehearsal ran overtime. Ethel Stark was such a perfectionist. It was now six thirty and Dora was at home, scrambling to get ready for the concert, which would be held at eight forty-five – a rather odd time, but it was what the women could get. There would be no time to fix her hair and make-up if she still hoped to grab a bite to eat. Besides, she wanted to polish her old French horn one more time. If only it would shine a little more. With a soft cloth she wiped it gently once again. No, it was still rather dull looking. But at least she could play it and make a rather nice sound.

With a small plate of food in one hand and an iron in the other, she rushed around her room, looking for her concert uniform.

"Aha! Here it is."

As she opened the box carefully, she recalled the last few months. The women had worked so hard. Would they withstand all the pressure? She unfolded the ironing board and spread out her concert uniform. What a beautiful sight. The long black gown with a white collar was simple but elegant. Ethel Stark had chosen the uniforms based on what the musicians wore in "serious" North American women's ensembles. The gown was a classic take on the traditional tuxedo that male musicians wore. Ethel did not want the women of her orchestra to look like fabricated dolls, the hyper-feminized women of the "Hour of Charm." Purchasing a uniform had been a bit of a financial sacrifice for some of the women, but now that she stared at herself in the mirror, Dora felt a sense of belonging, equality, and pride.

"Very professional," she complimented herself as she stared into the mirror.

It was now almost seven thirty, and she was running late. She had to go. Would her friends from the office come to the concert? What would they think? She wasn't sure if many people would show up, but her two sisters had promised to be there.

"So there will be at least two people in the audience," she thought, and giggled. She grabbed her instrument case and rushed out the door. She had to get up that mountain.

♫

On the other side of the city, Marie Brazeau was tuning her cello. The final dress rehearsal had tired her out, but it was now seven thirty and her new friend, violinist Helen Demuth, would be by shortly to pick her up. Marie couldn't possibly get up that mountain with her cello on her own, and certainly not this late in the evening. What a pity that she hadn't had time to take a short nap to rejuvenate a little. The dress rehearsal had been too long, but it was understandable since everyone was so excited and the inexperienced players had so many questions to ask.

"Patience," she muttered to herself as she struggled to tune the last string. Why was she tuning her cello now, anyway? She would have to re-tune it again in an hour.

Marie smiled to herself. She didn't want to admit it, but she was just a little nervous. She put the cello away, shut the case, and wheeled it to the front of her rooming house. There she sat on the front step, under a small fir tree, to wait for Helen. As she stared into the distance, she began to reminisce. She had always loved music. As a young woman she had wondered what it must be like to play for an audience as part of an orchestra. Tonight – at sixty years of age – she would finally live her dream.

"Marie! Marie!" Her friend's voice brought her attention back to the street where a car had pulled up. Helen, her husband, and children were here to take her up the mountain.

♫

Helen looked over with some admiration at her friend. The older woman looked so calm and collected. Surely, there was not an ounce of nerves in Marie. Helen, on the other hand, was very nervous and was trying hard not to show it. She was not a musician but a high school teacher, a wife and mother, and wasn't sure what to expect. She had never been on the concert stage. This would be her first time playing to an audience. Thankfully, Miss Stark had answered all her questions during the dress rehearsal earlier that afternoon: how to enter the stage, how to bow properly, and so on.

Marie and Helen didn't say much to each other during the car ride. They were grateful to Helen's husband and children for filling the silence with their chitchat.

♫

Violet Archer walked leisurely toward the Chalet, enjoying the cool breeze. She needed to unwind a little after all the commotion. Earlier that afternoon, the four MWSO percussionists had struggled with drums, cymbals, a xylophone, and various other instruments. When she had agreed to be second percussionist, she'd had no idea how much work it would entail in addition to playing.

"Steady!" May had yelled. "A little to the right…a little more… there." They had all puffed, trying to steady the xylophone. What a heavy instrument it was. In fact, the whole affair of assembling the stage had been quite the feat. And then there had been that dress rehearsal. Ethel had struggled not to lose her composure in the midst of all that nervous energy. They almost hadn't had enough time to rehearse Violet's arrangements of "God Save the King" and "O Canada," which the orchestra would be playing tonight. Now, she just needed time and space to collect her thoughts in silence.

"Violet!" called May. "Violet!"

No, there would be no time for quiet meditation. There was just too much excitement in the air.

♫

At eight thirty, the women of the MWSO gathered at the Chalet on top of Mount Royal. With its stunning view of the city, the Chalet was a popular recreational landmark for Montrealers and the perfect place to make a historic debut. The lights of the city glittered below, the evening breeze was cool, and the smell of fresh green grass filled the air. As they saw the crowd of people ascending the mountain, the women began to get nervous. Apart from a few players in the string sections, such as Gertrude Probyn and Lotte Goetzel, most of them had never set foot on a concert stage. They had little idea about the proper decorum or how to handle nerves

The MWSO's debut concert was a roaring success. Two thousand people had to be turned away, while five thousand enjoyed the program inside the Chalet, which still stands atop Mount Royal today.

in the public eye. And now here they were, seven months in, and giving a public concert to hundreds…no, thousands, of people!

To everyone's delight, an astonishing five thousand people turned up and another two thousand were turned away. The orchestra members' relatives, who were acting as ushers, were not quite sure how to handle the situation. Security had to be called in to manage the crowds. Those who arrived too late and couldn't get a view of the orchestra sat on the grass to listen to the music. But there was one girl who had reached the Chalet early and had a front-row seat: Violet Louise Grant.

The other Violet – Violet Archer – paced back and forth backstage. Under the encouragement of Miss Stark, she had arranged two pieces for tonight's debut: "O Canada" and "God Save the King." What if people didn't like her arrangements? She was a "woman composer" after all. A tap on the shoulder from May told her it was time to go onstage.

At last the women entered the stage and began to warm up their instruments. They looked elegant in their simple black dresses with white collars, their faces shining with great anticipation. Mildred, the concertmistress, was so excited that she almost forgot to tune the orchestra, but a look from the oboist, Lois, who had traveled from New York for the debut concert, reminded her the time had come. Everyone tuned her instrument as well as she could, with the more experienced players giving subtle hints to those whose hearing was suddenly overcome by nerves. Madge Bowen sat in the violin section, looking pleased and holding her instrument tightly – this would be her first performance with a symphony orchestra, at the age of fifty-four. She glanced over at her daughter, Margaret, who had taken her place by the piano, and they smiled at each other. Madge's dream was unfolding beyond her wildest expectations. At last, when Ethel Stark entered the stage wearing a stunning white dress with a glittering gold belt, the performers stood up and there was thunderous applause.

"When I entered the stage from the wings of the chalet and saw the sea of faces, and the panoramic, magnificent scene in front of me, and turned to the orchestra which was set up beautifully, with a concert grand piano on each side of the stage, I simply could not control my emotions and tears came to my eyes," Ethel recalled.

Ethel acknowledged the crowd, gave the signal, and the music began. The orchestra opened with Violet Archer's renditions of "God Save the King" and "O Canada," followed by a piece by Beethoven. Ethel conducted the orchestra with fierce determination. In the intense climatic moments that required burly musical power, she looked like a savage beast waiting to pounce, and in the moments where the melodies drifted sweetly, her demeanor changed to that of a child having a vision of angels. Ethel's face was so expressive.

"[I've] got to show the orchestra, I've got to show it with my face…with my eyes, with my whole being, and with my hands to develop it…and then they react," she explained. Indeed, Ethel

Stark had a wonderful gift for communicating to her players what she wanted and how she wanted it done with a simple look, a wave, or a grand gesture. Captivated, the players forgot how nervous they were and concentrated on making beautiful music. Yes, this was *real* music.

Intertwined with the soaring melodies, the intense harmonies, and the infectious rhythms, there was a different kind of noise: a

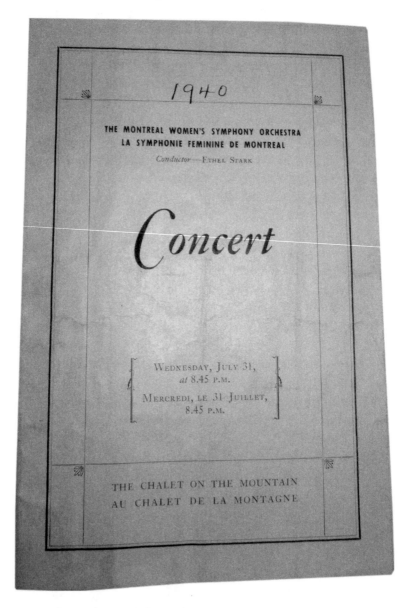

clatter created by the movement of curious onlookers who wanted to see women playing "manly" musical instruments. Chairs were shuffled, bodies shifted, people began to whisper to each other. Was it true they had been playing together for only seven months? Could a woman really play a French horn? And look at that violinist: she's pregnant! (Indeed, the violinist was due in four days.)[36]

The program for the first public concert, listed Violet Archer's arrangements.

The next piece was a popular work by J.S. Bach. The audience watched with incredulity as the musicians performed the entire piece from memory. While it is not uncommon to see maestros conduct from memory, it is rather novel to witness an ensemble of musicians perform anything from memory. Keeping together as an ensemble is difficult enough while keeping an eye on the conductor and keeping an eye on the score. Playing from memory takes considerable skill, concentration, and cooperation, not to mention the many hours of work that have to go into memorizing notes, dynamics, rhythms, and countless other signs and symbols. The message the orchestra sent this night was clear: This was no ordinary orchestra, and the women were not just there to play for recreation. They were going to become a professional orchestra, and soon.

In fact, from the very beginning Ethel was absolutely convinced that her orchestra of amateurs would in time become an eminent professional music ensemble ranking alongside the best orchestras in the country. She firmly believed that this all-female orchestra would enhance an appreciation and awareness of women's music-making in Montreal, in Canada, and even around the world. Never for a moment did she think it was anything but entirely possible. This concert was only a small proof that women musicians could deliver artistic results on par with male ensembles.

Mozart's "Paris" Symphony came next, followed by Saint-Saens's *Le Carnaval des Animaux* with Sonia Slatin (billed as "Sandra Slatin" this evening), as one of the featured pianists. Sonia was thrilled to be in Montreal, playing with the only all-woman symphony orchestra on the continent.

As the music soared, curious tolerance turned into admiration. When the concert finished, the public gave the orchestra a rousing ovation. The applause and cheers went on and on.

"It was an enchanting evening of sheer magic for us because everything fell into place, as if destiny had acted for us," recalled Ethel. It was, indeed, a very dramatic debut for the orchestra and especially for Madge, Doretta, and Ethel, who had worked so hard.

Young Violet Louise Grant rooted for an encore. She was ecstatic. Besides being her first live symphony orchestra concert, this event had also shown her that stereotypes could be defeated. If women could play "manly" instruments, black people could play "white-collar" instruments as well. They could be part of a symphony orchestra too. More than anything, however, Violet Louise was simply thrilled with the idea of an orchestra for women of all backgrounds. Would Miss Stark accept a black woman as a regular and permanent member of her all-white symphony orchestra?

Violet Louise's concerns were not unfounded. Like women, blacks were originally excluded from major symphony orchestras in North America. Although there were many black jazz musicians, discrimination and limited access to musical training were largely responsible for the shortage of African-American performers of classical music. To combat the exclusion, many formed their own segregated orchestras to provide training and support. Occasionally, high-profile black musicians would appear in the traditionally white world of "high art" music, but this tokenism was also tinged with a racist motivation to juxtapose an "exotic" black body against a sea of white ones. It wasn't until 1948 that the first major symphony orchestra in North America, the Los Angeles Philharmonic, hired a black musician – contrabassist Henry Lewis. This however, did not break all prejudices. When the Symphony of the Air orchestra tried to hire three African-American players for one of its concerts in the 1950s, a white member protested by walking out and threatening to withdraw from the final performance.[37] But this was 1940, and as of yet no major orchestra in the US or Canada had hired a black musician on a permanent basis. Would the Montreal Women's Symphony Orchestra be an integrated group? Could this orchestra be the exception to the norm, even if there was to be no pay?

"I have to be part of that orchestra," Violet Louise thought to herself. "But how?" She was black, she was poor, she could not play an orchestral instrument, and even if she could, she didn't have one.

"You want to join an orchestra?" her father said when she told him her idea that night. "You'll find a way!"

As she lay in bed, Violet Louise came up with a plan: She would continue her music studies as a pianist, teach some music lessons, and earn enough money to purchase an orchestral instrument.

She would gather up the courage to ask for membership into the traditionally white world of the symphony orchestra. Her goal was to become a member of the first and only all-woman symphony orchestra in Canada.

♪

Reviews appeared in the papers the day after the debut concert. One critic claimed that the MWSO concert had been an immense success and that he hoped the orchestra would perform more concerts in the future.[38] He went on to say that the Bach suite, which was performed from memory, "was played with very good tone and rhythm."[39] Violet Archer was pleased he acknowledged that her arrangements of "God Save the King" and "O Canada" were "a decided improvement on that which is usually played."[40] Music critic Thomas Archer observed that the group was an "admirably disciplined ensemble, one that can give a clear intelligent performance of a score; an ensemble that above all plays with an enthusiasm which cannot fail to communicate itself to the audience."[41]

Over wine and cheese at Madge Bowen's house, the women of the orchestra toasted their achievement. The Montreal Women's Symphony Orchestra was here to stay.

CHAPTER SIX
Crescendo

Considering its humble beginnings with a penny-pinching budget, old instruments needing repairs, and inexperienced players (not to mention a rat-infested basement with set of broken chairs for a rehearsal hall), the orchestra's first year had been a grand success. Despite their triumphant debut, the women knew there was still a lot of work ahead of them. Ethel Stark was determined to prove that the musical success of the first concert was not isolated and better performances were yet to come.

By 1941 the orchestra had played six concerts that were received relatively well. Ethel was pleased with the constant improvement and gradually diminished the frequency of rehearsals from a frantic five times a week to what would eventually become the norm, once a week. Because most women were housewives or worked during the day, the rehearsals had to be held at night when everyone was tired. Violet Archer recalled, "we had to go whenever everybody could come to the rehearsal, so it had to be at night, and I would be so tired after a long day of going from one house to another, teaching my piano students."[42]

The sheer joy of playing music, being around other like-minded women, having someone believe in their abilities, and

Doretta Stark (second from left), Ethel, and Madge Bowen (fourth and fifth from left) met with the organizing committee for the MWSO's 1940 concert at Verdun Hall.

performing every few months made the long hours of practice worthwhile. The women hummed the tunes they would play that night as they worked in the factories and offices and stole away during the lunch hour to study their scores. The idea of playing music, of forgetting their troubles in the making of contagious melodies and beautiful harmonies gave them the strength to persevere through the day. It was truly refreshing and rewarding to be a musician.

Lyse Vézina recalls,

> It was nice because…[a]nyone who wanted to could be in the orchestra…but she had to know her instrument and her music well before coming to rehearsals. There were a few professional musicians, but there were also women that had other occupations: housewives, secretaries, nurses. There were even mothers of little children and their husbands, who had to watch the children, while they were away at rehearsals. Everybody had fun together. We went there to relax, to play, to enjoy ourselves. It was nice and encouraging, even for those of us who were taking private music lessons. We were making beautiful music…it was the chance of a lifetime. There was no other women's orchestra in the world conducted by a woman.

Despite their diligent attempts to create a professional orchestra – a serious orchestra – the frequent references of the press to the members' "femininity," that is, their amateur, recreational, and social (rather than professional) status, was irritating. Such references undermined their hard work, commitment, skill, and triumphs. The press wondered: Did these women discuss hobbies, their husbands, or children during rehearsals? Did they have tea? Did they knit while waiting for their turn? Over the years, the women reassured the press again and again that during rehearsals they worked just as hard as any other orchestra. Sometimes they used the language that critics would understand, in particular "business-like." Ethel once assured a reporter, "There's no gossip about teas or clothes or babies or recipes. They mean business."[43] During a speech at a conference, Ethel stressed once again that the women did indeed work hard and attentively during rehearsals. She said:

> A visit to one of our rehearsals, which are not as a rule "closed" affairs, will show a group of seventy studious, musically-minded women at work taking orders and taking directions from a leader who is naturally strung to the highest nervous pitch, and who has little time to remember always all the little politenesses [sic]. The visitor would see a serious group going through the painstaking work of rehearsal – that necessary workout in which maddening repetition takes on glamour for the sincere enthusiast, for it is that that works for perfection. The members of our orchestra go through all this unflinchingly, and even gladly, because results have been forthcoming in performance, and because there is a sense of achievement and promise of better things for an organization which is the only one of its kind on the Continent.[44]

In fact, playing in a symphony orchestra was not something the women took for granted. It was a privilege. Second percussionist Violet Archer, for example, attended every rehearsal, even those she wasn't required to attend. Aspiring to become a full-time professional composer, Violet used every opportunity to learn about musical styles and repertoire. She purchased all the scores that the

MWSO played for its concerts and used the lengthy periods where she didn't have to play to follow along, study, and memorize all the main melodies. In 1993 a journalist with CBC Radio asked her if she really had bought all the scores, to which she replied:

> Oh yes, all the stuff that the orchestra played; I got myself a score. I sat – in fact, I would go to those rehearsals and I would memorize the principal themes whenever it was a symphony – because that orchestra did all the standard repertoire, all the Brahms and Beethoven, Haydn, Mozart, William Walton, César Franck, Tchaikovsky, of course, and I would listen and try to identify the principal themes and memorize them, and I would go home and write them down. (I still have my notebooks in a box downstairs.) Then I would get the score. I would look at the score and see if I had it right or not.[45]

The journalist then asked her if she had a lot of time as a percussionist to count bars and to study the music, to which she replied jokingly, "Oh, I did nothing else," referring to the long periods of rest that second percussionists often have in their music. Violet was there to work hard. She would not take this precious opportunity for granted.

The MWSO also supported Violet Archer's development as a composer. In 1942, the orchestra performed her "Tone Poem: Leaves of Grass" and in 1946 it premiered her "Sea Drift for Chorus and Orchestra." Violet later recalled, "We played some of my music...I remember that. From a suite called *Leaves of Grass*, of Walton Whitman. When I first discovered that book, I was just crazy about it. I read it from cover to cover. And I wrote a big suite for women's voices and orchestra and they played two different movements of it at two different concerts."[46]

There were other women who were working hard to become professional musicians and for whom the orchestra was an important part of their training and experience. Lyse Vézina recalls, "For me, [the orchestra] was part of my development.... It was a chance to learn the repertoire. There were a few of us who were on the point of becoming professionals. We were seated at the front."

Because Ethel knew how important the orchestra was to all the women, regardless of their individual situation, she poured her heart and soul into the experience of building a professional ensemble. An important part of becoming professional was creating musical programs that would be simultaneously educational for the musicians, gratifying for the audiences, and beneficial to the community at large. Ethel Stark's connections with the many celebrities she had mingled with in Philadelphia and New York were now useful. Not surprisingly, the majority of guest soloists were Jewish; Ethel was very proud of her own heritage and supported the Jewish community. She was also a recipient of their constant support. These soloists included Ethel's long-time teacher and friend, Lea Luboshutz, as well as past friends and acquaintances such as pianist, conductor, and opera commentator Boris Goldovsky (whom she had met as a student at the artists' colony in Maine), pianist Nadia Reinsenberg, Canadian cellist Zara Nelsova, violinist Benno Rabinof, and American composer and pianist Percy Grainger, among others. Guest soloists seldom charged the orchestra for their services or would accept only travel fees. The Bowen family generously hosted many of the soloists who were personal friends of Ethel Stark at their Laurentian estate, and the celebrations would continue into the late hours of the night. Madge's granddaughter Ann remembers quite vividly that on one occasion Percy Grainger practiced with such vigor that one of the keys flew off their piano.

Energetic performances, famous guest artists, varied programming, and

New Work Will Be Heard Next Week

OCT · 1940

The tone poem composed by Violet Archer which is to be included by Miss Stark in the concert of the Montreal Women's Symphony Orchestra concert next Wednesday, is taken from Walt Whitman's "Leaves of Grass." It is the poem, "Song of the Universal," and at the time of its publication was heralded as something so new that it was difficult to understand.

The theme of the poem is the familiar one that out of all turmoil, and in spite of the discord of human struggle, there is a rhythm which we all obey. An idea which might be expressed more freely, probably, in music than in words. The style of Miss Archer's work is inclined to be modal, which matches the spirit of Walt Whitman's verse. The music requires a full ochestra and is written especially for female voices.

Miss Stark, who was impressed by the work after Miss Archer, who is one of the musicians in the orchestra, had described it to her, has succeeded in finding and training forty women for the part. It is not in the ordinary sense of the word, a piece of music in which voices and orchestra are two separate separate parts; the voices are interwoven into the whole pattern.

Miss Archer was born in Montreal, and was a scholar of the McGill Conservatorium.

Violet Archer's compositions were featured works in the MWSO repertoire.

American composer Percy Grainger was a guest artist with the MWSO. Staying with the Bowens while in Montreal, he practiced on their piano so forcefully that one of the keys flew off.

novelty repertoire were all part of the MWSO concert experience. Some concerts introduced new works never before performed in Canada, while others highlighted more traditional classical repertoire. There were concerts with renowned soloists who frequented the world's most prestigious concert halls, and there were concerts that introduced Montreal's young budding talent. And there were also the odd haphazard performances and situations bordering on the hilarious.

♫

Ethel and the orchestra were thrilled that virtuoso violinist Benno Rabinof would perform for their spring concert on May 7, 1942. Mr. Rabinof had prepared Paganini's technically dazzling Violin Concerto in D Major. The evening of the concert came and players made their way to the theater for the dress rehearsal. As soloists often volunteered their time, dress rehearsals were very limited, very short, and sometimes took place only hours before the actual performance – a hazardous venture for any orchestra, but especially one with such a short history of playing together. The margin for error was very small.

It was during this already musically perilous occasion that members discovered their featured soloist had learned the concerto in a different key from the one they had rehearsed – soloist and orchestra had essentially two different sounding scores. His solo part was in D major, but the orchestral version was scored in E-flat major. In the original version, Paganini had written instructions

The only symphony orchestra in North America composed entirely of women and directed by a woman.

THE MONTREAL WOMEN'S SYMPHONY ORCHESTRA

ETHEL STARK
Conductor
Patron: His Excellency the Governor General of Canada

PLATEAU HALL
WEDNESDAY, OCT. 15th, at 8.30

Tickets: Orchestra $3.00, 2.25, 2.00
Balcony $2.25, 2.00, 1.25

Phone HA. 5536, Room 311,
Dominion Square Bldg.

One of the first photos of the MWSO, taken at Montreal's Plateau Hall, where several of the orchestra's early concerts were held.

to tune the violin a semitone higher. However, Rabinof had been given a modern version in which both the orchestra and violin parts are transposed to D major and he did not practice the piece with a different tuning. He could, perhaps, retune his violin, but he had memorized the music in D major and it was apparent that simply re-tuning the violin would cause him much inconvenience for he now heard the entire piece, including the orchestra's part, in D major. Ethel could not possibly ask her guest to take the brunt of what was ultimately her mistake; she had rented the wrong scores. What could be done about this terrible mix up?

"There is only one solution," said Ethel. "The orchestra members will have to transpose their parts." And turning to the orchestra, baton in hand, she commanded, "You have fifteen minutes."

Learning a Paganini concerto at any given moment is difficult, but when an entire orchestra has to transpose a twenty-four minute score to accommodate the soloist only hours before the concert, it is almost incredible. Some members panicked, some chuckled nervously, and some thought Ethel was out of her mind; but when it came time to perform, no one in the audience was able to notice the stress the women were under. Rabinof commended their professionalism and Thomas Archer of the *Montreal Gazette* claimed that had he not been aware of the handicap, he would not have noticed. Only a team with an adventurous and unwavering spirit could have pulled it off.

But the drama did not end there. The piece that followed was Herbert Haufrecht's *Ferdinand the Bull*, based on the story by Munro Leaf about a bull that prefers to spend his time smelling flowers rather than fighting matadors. The New York Philharmonic Orchestra (NYPO) had given the world premiere of this piece the previous year, and Ethel thought it would be rather fun to play on a program and a good piece to introduce in Canada. It was full of surprises that involved many interesting sounds. It was sure to engross the younger members of the audience.

Percussionist Violet Archer recalled with some amusement how she played an array of trinkets for this delightful musical comedy. "I played, among other things, a cow bell. And also, we borrowed an instrument from the New York Philharmonic, which, when you blew into it, sounded like the moo of a cow. And of course, I had to do that. Oh, I had fun. I enjoyed it."[47]

There is one particular part in the piece when the matador makes his entrance to the shouting of "Olé! Olé!" by the orchestra members. It was a section they had rehearsed over and over again to avoid accidents and miscalculations – it would have been an embarrassment if a lone member bellowed into the packed auditorium by herself.

Everything was going well during the performance until Ethel became so genuinely excited waiting for the big moment when the matador enters that she got a few bars ahead of the orchestra. Suddenly and without warning, she threw her head back, waved her arms in the air and all by herself confidently shrieked in a thunderous voice, "Olé! Olé! Olé!"

It was hilarious. The silliness of it almost caused a train wreck as the musicians and conductor scrambled to hide their laughter. Mildred caught Ethel's eye and could barely contain herself. Dora pretended to cough while she buried her face in her sleeve; some violinists bit their tongues to hide their smiles; the flutist seemed as if she would lose her grip on her instrument; the oboist did almost drop hers. The more desperately they tried to stifle their giggles, the worse it became. Eventually, everyone was overcome. Stark turned red but kept on conducting.

"Everyone was literally in stitches and it took considerable will power to stand up there and continue conducting while shaking with laughter," recalled Ethel.

Thankfully, there were so many musical jokes in the piece that Stark's lonesome hollering and the giggling musicians became part of this first rate entertainment. The Canadian debut of this original piece of music was a grand success. Thomas Archer reported that "the audience chuckled and laughed last night, enjoying the joke hugely."

Laughing seemed to come naturally to the women in the orchestra, but giggling fits were not the only unexpected reactions that temporarily threatened their music making. On another occasion during a performance of Leopold Mozart's "Toy Symphony" at a children's concert, the flutist had a plastic quail that had to be filled with water and blown into in order to "sing." No expertise or practice was needed to make this gimmick work. But during the concert, the flutist began to have doubts. She grew so nervous about her "solo" that when the time came for the quail to sing, she blew into it with so much force that water sprayed all over the unsuspecting members of the woodwind section. The surprised look on their soaked faces almost made the other players dissolve into another fit of laughter.

♫

Spontaneous joy permeated the music making of the MWSO members, especially in their public performances. But, when it was time to work during rehearsals they were all business. Yes, rehearsals were quite a different matter. At the *tap, tap* of Ethel's baton, a deafening silence fell. The women waited for the maestra's instructions.

"Ethel was demanding, she knew what she wanted. She got the utmost out of the group of women…she was very strong and bossy. What she said had to be," recalls Pearl Aronoff.

"Miss Stark was very strict," another member confirms. "Very, very strict and precise. She was in charge. There were some people who came, played for a while, and then left because they thought she was too strict."

"Sometimes funny things would happen," adds Lyse Vézina. "We would laugh, but only a little because Ethel was very serious and very strict. Sometimes she was a bit feisty. She had plenty of character."

Ethel commanded her ship with confidence and authority. She was fair, showed no favoritism, and would accept nothing but the best. Sometimes, Ethel would become infuriated at what she considered a lack of preparation from some of the members. It didn't matter whether the musician had been playing for three years or ten years, whether she was the wife of a wealthy executive or a worker in the munitions factory. It didn't matter whether she was black or white, English or French, Jewish or Christian. Sometimes, Ethel would stop rehearsals with a heavy sigh. She would single out each offending musician and they would have to play through their individual parts in front of everyone else, one by one. Faces flushed bright red, knees turned to jelly, and palms became sweaty. No one could hide her laziness from Ethel Stark. Even Madge Bowen ceased to become the president of the organization during rehearsals and concerts and became just another member of the violin section, taking orders and paying "for each technical error via the corrective abuse handed out, without fear or favor" by their conductor.[48] As violinist Mary Machim later said of her leader, "It was amazing what [Ethel Stark] did for us. She was a very fine musician who allowed no sloppiness to go unchallenged. If she heard wrongdoings, she could roar like a lion.... Stark knew what she wanted and demanded enough to make you work very hard. Playing under her was a great challenge."[49]

Ethel could not only "roar like a lion" on the podium but act like one as well. At times she would strike her baton on the stand so hard that it seemed it would splinter. When she heard wrong notes, her eyes would shoot flames. When she couldn't communicate what she wanted musically to the orchestra, she berated herself. Despite her occasional fits of anger, the women loved and respected their conductor. In fact, if the women were so committed and devoted to the orchestra, it was only because they saw in Ethel a good role model – a highly disciplined musician devoted to her artistic goals. Feisty Ethel was a visionary, an innovator, and a mover and shaker. She was constantly raising the level of playing of the MWSO musicians. Even in just the first couple of years, she had accomplished much with the orchestra.

In 1942, however, Ethel received a crushing blow. Her father passed away from cancer and her mother became ill, making Ethel the breadwinner for the family. Bills came in for the doctor, chemotherapy treatments, medicine, rent, food, and numerous other expenses. As the orchestra brought her no steady income, Ethel had to take on an additional thirty hours of teaching per week, in addition to giving solo performances. It was a situation that fatigued her severely. She wanted a rest, but when Madge invited her and Doretta to vacation with her family and other members of the orchestra, the Stark sisters declined.

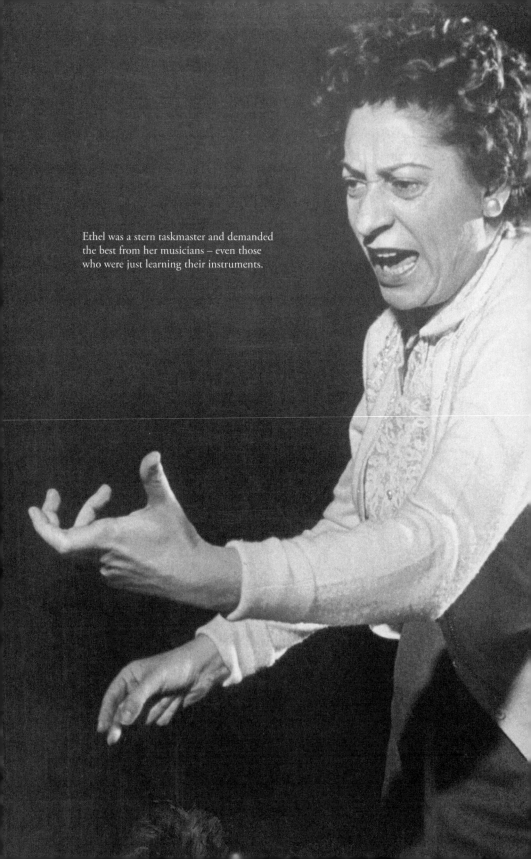

Ethel was a stern taskmaster and demanded
the best from her musicians – even those
who were just learning their instruments.

The Bowens had a lovely summer home in Lac Écho, which consisted of a main home and five cottages. Here, they would host some of the guest performers of the MWSO and invite members of the orchestra for parties, holidays, and relaxation. The following year, Madge again invited the Stark sisters to her summer cottage to relax, but again they declined. One day, Doretta finally told Madge that they would love to go but could not leave their mother alone.

"Take one of the cottages and bring your mother!" replied Madge. The invitation was accepted with pleasure and the sisters spent a lovely time in a beautiful two-bedroom cottage overlooking the lake. Madge even supplied them with a housekeeper who was an excellent gourmet cook. As Ethel's frail mother regained her strength, Ethel was able to relax, study her scores, and practice the violin.

Other members of the orchestra occupied some of the other cabins. Perceived barriers were broken and lifelong connections and friendships were cemented on these special outings.

In a genuine spirit of hospitality, when Sunday mornings came Madge would get in the boat and row the French-speaking Roman Catholic members of the orchestra across the lake to a Catholic Mass and then hurry back across the lake and drive the English-speaking Anglican members on the rocky roads to the Anglican service. In the afternoon, she drove the Yiddish-speaking Jewish women to do their shopping at a kosher butcher shop in Shawbridge.

Gertrude Probyn, the orchestra's double bassist, and violinist Mrs. John Pratt were frequent guests at the Bowens' summer villa. Elderly Gertrude Probyn particularly loved entertaining Madge's grandchildren, putting on plays for them and performing music outdoors. A piano would be hauled onto the patio and the women would organize themselves into duos, trios, or quartets and play in the cool breeze under the sun.

"I remember one particular rainy day. It rained all day and the children were restless," recalled Madge's granddaughter. "Mrs. Probyn and the other musicians put on a show for us – *Peter and the Wolf* – and we laughed and laughed to see them acting it out."

Madge Bowen was not only the ideal president of a pioneering women's organization, but also a kind, generous person and dedicated citizen overall. Described as "a tireless worker," "a social leader," and "the heart and soul" of the orchestra, she was not someone who loved the spotlight;[50] she preferred to work behind the scenes. If the orchestra was a budding flower, Ethel was its gardener and Madge its water and sun. Without Madge, the vision to create an inclusive orchestra of women would not have bloomed as it did.

♪

The orchestra's rapid progress pleased both Ethel and Madge, but what satisfied them even more was knowing that its mission of inclusivity was one of the most significant benefits of all, especially for women who would not otherwise have a chance to play classical music in the public eye. It was, therefore, a pleasant surprise when in 1943, Joseph Moretti, the clarinet professor at the Quebec Conservatory of Music, asked Ethel Stark to audition one of his students, a young black woman named Violet Louise Grant. He explained that she had only started playing clarinet a few months earlier, but he felt she had exceptional potential. Ethel and Madge couldn't help feeling especially pleased that this young woman was reaching out to their orchestra. The Starks were good friends with a black family who lived next door and Ethel was well aware of their experiences. She understood what a determined person this young clarinet player must be. Yes, she and Madge told Professor Moretti, the orchestra needed another clarinet player. They would be happy to audition Violet Louise.

After attending the concert debut of the MWSO on top of Mount Royal, Violet Louise couldn't stop talking about the orchestra, and soon her entire family began to share her enthusiasm. Violet's younger sister, Joyce, was in sixth grade at the time and recalls a particular MWSO concert on December 26, 1942, when the entire family crammed into the cold streetcar and headed up to the Hermitage for a young people's concert – it was like a Christmas present for the entire family. Both girls were delighted by the "elephant" piece played on the double bass by Gertrude Probyn. She moved to the middle of stage with her huge instrument and began to play the part of an elephant. The children in the audience couldn't stop laughing; it was too much fun.

Violet Louise couldn't wait to be a part of this orchestra, but she had no opportunity to learn an orchestral instrument yet. Then one day in 1943 her brother came home with exciting news about a new school of music, the Quebec Conservatory of Music, which provided free music lessons to talented students – and they were looking for students to fill their quota. Violet Louise wasted no time applying as a pianist, and as soon as she was accepted, she asked if it was possible to learn an orchestral instrument instead.

When Violet Louise Grant was eighty-seven years old, she was asked why, out of all the instruments in the orchestra, she had chosen to play the clarinet.

"Because it was the cheapest instrument I could find!" she exclaimed, laughing heartily. "I asked the secretary if I could play a woodwind instrument instead of the piano, and when she asked me what instrument I wanted to play, I said, 'Depends what the cheapest one is!' My family had no money to buy a new instrument. One of my friends was a clarinet player and she got tired of it. She wanted to sell it for fifty dollars. The instrument was not in great condition and needed many repairs. One of the keys kept getting stuck and I had to keep lifting it up!"

After mimicking how she held the clarinet with the sticky key she continued, "Squeak, squawk, toot! That's what it was like in the beginning!" She laughed. "But I kept going.... My father worked on the railroad. When he came home he was very tired; always the first day home we were quiet in the house, so there was no way I could be practicing – too too ti ti!.... My family had to put up with all the squawking coming from that clarinet!"

Now the day of the audition was finally here. Violet felt as if she had been practicing for this all her life – a chance to play in an orchestra! She arrived promptly for her audition, greeted Miss Stark rather shyly, warmed up her battered instrument, and waited for the cue. After a deep breath, she closed her eyes and began to play through her pieces. When she was finished, she put down her instrument and waited for what seemed an eternity. Ethel's response was music to Violet's ears: "Good. Come back next week." Violet was now a member of the Montreal Women's Symphony Orchestra.

"Playing in the orchestra...was just the thrill of a lifetime," she recalled. "For me it was seventh heaven sitting there playing all this music that I love so much." Moreover, in the MWSO no one treated her differently, no one mentioned her skin color, and for the first time in a long time she felt accepted and challenged. "There was never any reference to color or race in the orchestra. It wasn't so much a relief, it was just such a thrill, such a blessing. With Miss Stark there was only one thing that mattered, making sure you knew your score. It wasn't teatime!"

Violet Louise's membership in the MWSO marked the first time that a black Canadian played in a Canadian symphony orchestra on a permanent basis. The MWSO became the first racially integrated complete symphony orchestra devoted to the playing of "classical" or "concert" music in Canada, and quite possibly in North America.[51] The civil rights movement of the 1960s opened up many doors for black musicians, and by the end of the decade several orchestras, including the New York Symphony of the New World and the Quebec Symphony Orchestra, provided opportunities for many black instrumentalists. But almost twenty years earlier, the Montreal Women's Symphony Orchestra had succeeded in breaking down the color barrier. At the time, Violet Louise was unaware of the significance of her social achievement; she was simply focused on the experience of playing in an orchestra and the sheer joy of making music.

The Grant family was extremely proud of their daughter, and despite their poverty, they always tried to support Violet Louise's endeavors with the women's orchestra. "My father loved classical music, especially orchestral music," Violet recalls. "We would all sit around the old radio and listen for hours. On Saturday mornings there was a program for young people, and we would listen to the opera too. My father would pass the radio around. Oh, it was wonderful!" When her father was home, he would take the family to the concerts. Her sister Joyce would rush home from school, do her homework, eat supper, and the family would head off to Plateau Hall, where many concerts were held throughout the years. Violet Louise's involvement with the orchestra brought them in contact with many talented musicians.

Violet Louise Grant, a talented young pianist, joined the MWSO as a clarinetist. She was the first black Canadian to play in a symphony orchestra on a permanent basis.

In the 1940s, the Grants likely struck some people as odd for their affinity to "high culture" music. They were, after all, considered part of the "lower" socioeconomic classes. Violet Louise Grant was a trailblazer who proved that given the chance, black musicians could perform classical music in a symphony orchestra. The orchestra's inclusivity and Violet's accomplishment was noted by the *Negro Digest* of Montreal.

For the other women in the orchestra, having Violet Louise was a blessing, especially since woodwind players were hard to come by. Slowly, the ensemble was expanding in size and in color.

Playing together, week after week, year after year, created in the musicians a sense of responsibility, of solidarity and *esprit de corps*.

This was "their" orchestra. Being a part of this orchestra of women had its advantages. They were not hindered by male bureaucracy that dictated how they should operate nor encumbered by male chauvinism that tried to present them as entertainers – or as sex objects. Men did not manage them; they managed themselves. Men did not play music for them; they played their own. Men did not intimidate them; here the women felt free. Yes, the music was theirs, the space was theirs, the playing was theirs. They were a family.

♫

It was now December 1, 1943, and the women were putting on the final touches for the evening concert featuring the music of Beethoven, Holst, and Bruch. Madge was thrilled to be playing one of her favorite pieces of music – Beethoven's Symphony No. 3, the "Eroica." Dora was equally excited, as the piece features a prominent French horn part. During the dress rehearsal, however, she suddenly fell ill with a fever. Dora did not mind missing time from the office, but she knew she could not miss a concert with the MWSO. Besides, who could possibly replace her this late in the day? There weren't many women in Montreal who could play the French horn.

"I can't let the entire ensemble down," she thought. After all, they were like family.

When Ethel took one look at Dora – pale, lethargic, and shivering with chills – she knew something was very wrong.

"Go home and get well," said Ethel, but Dora insisted on remaining for the concert and refused to step down from her place on the stage despite her alarmingly high fever. Ethel was not one to backpedal once she'd given an order, but when she saw that Dora's determination stemmed from a sincere desire to help rather than from any kind of ego, she consented with one condition. Dora agreed and a doctor was called in. He sternly warned her that if she did not rest, her illness could escalate. Still, Dora persisted. During the concert the doctor stood backstage, ready to treat her in case of an emergency. As soon as the last notes of the music drifted into silence and Ethel lowered her baton, Dora grabbed her instrument and rushed off to bed. She didn't even wait for the applause to end. Like many of her other sisters in music, Dora's commitment to the group's mission remained strong through the years.

♪

Sacrificing for the ensemble was key to keeping it in operation, whether it was forgoing evenings with family for practices, investing personal funds for music lessons, offering a kitchen or living room for sectional rehearsals, or lending a hand in other ways. Occasionally, the women who were better off financially would organize a "big drive" for major concerts in order to provide rides for those who needed transportation. Elderly cellist Marie Brazeau and double bassist Gertrude Probyn were especially grateful. But on one occasion, the organizers of the "big drive" made a big mistake.

The 1944–45 season seemed rather gloomy. It had been a terribly cold fall, the winter seemed to have lasted longer than usual, and the spring brought rain, rain, and more rain. Dragging instruments all across the city week after week was tiresome, especially in the biting wind, freezing rain, and mushy snow.

The "big drive" organizers had arranged to pick up Ethel at her home and drop her off at Plateau Hall for an evening concert. Peeking from behind the living room curtains for what seemed the hundredth time and squinting as hard as she could to see into the distance, Ethel wondered why her ride was not already here. The sky was dark, the wind blew ferociously, and rain was pelting forcefully. A sudden flash of lightning and a clap of thunder startled Ethel back into her chair.

"What a terrible storm," she thought. "Imagine having to walk in this weather."

She sensed that something was seriously wrong. Doretta was already at the concert hall, managing the setup, ticket sales, and all the other duties that came with the job of orchestra manager. In fact, by now people would likely be lining up outside the hall buying tickets. She had to find a way to Plateau Hall somehow.

Once again she peered outside in the hopes of finding a familiar face. Seeing no one, she grabbed her trench coat and umbrella and headed out into the rain, yelling frantically when she spotted a taxi.

"Drive as fast as possible to Plateau Hall," she instructed. She arrived minutes before the doors opened to the public. Clutching her umbrella, she scampered around to the backstage door.

"At last!" she thought. But the door was locked. *Pound! Pound! Pound!* She hammered on the door as forcefully as she could. Getting no response, she raced to the front of the hall. After fighting her way through the crowd, she came to the main door where a policeman was guarding the entrance.

"Excuse me! I must get in at once!" She was panting as she pushed her way forward. The guard extended his brawny arm to block her.

"No, you don't!" he said. "No one is allowed in until the orchestra manager gives the cue. I have explicit instructions."

"I am the conductor," Ethel snapped.

"I don't care who you are! Those are my orders."

Ethel's eyes flashed. What a foolish man! He was forbidding her to enter her own concert!

"There will be no concert unless I get through!"

"Madame, to the back of the line. I am not letting you through."

In desperation, Ethel lunged back into the pouring rain. She plowed through the thick mud, hauling her belongings after her as she lifted her heels forcefully to prevent them from sinking. Frantically, she pounded even harder on the backstage door, yelling for someone to open.

Meanwhile, inside Plateau Hall, the musicians were beginning to wonder what had happened to their conductor and what was going to happen to them if she didn't show up. A violinist on her way to the washroom heard someone pounding madly on the door – should she open it? What if it was someone trying to break in?

"Oh, use the front door!" she thought and ignored the pounding. But on her way out of the washroom there was that constant banging. Cautiously, she opened the door an inch and peered out.

There stood her conductor, drenched and covered in mud, her dark curls dangling over her face.

This 1945 concert at Plateau Hall almost didn't happen. Ethel was late arriving and refused admittance by a policeman at the door to the hall.

That night, the performers barely recognized their leader, who always took particular care with her appearance on stage. But the flat, damp curls and lack of make-up didn't seem to affect the music. The concert was still a grand success.

♫

There were indeed many comical moments in the life of the MWSO, and these helped to keep the women's spirits alive during darker times – and with the war in Europe, there were indeed dark times for various orchestra members. One late summer day in 1945, just as the war was on the brink of ending, Ethel received news: Her sweetheart had been sent to Italy on a final mission with two other soldiers. An enemy torpedo hit their plane and they perished almost instantly. Ethel was devastated. But she kept her pain private, and with Doretta's companionship, she slowly recovered and was able to fully focus on her work and her future.

Ethel continued to thrive as a solo violinist and experienced several highlights of her own. She played numerous recitals for CBC Radio and appeared as soloist with the CBC Symphony Orchestra, the Little Symphonies, Les Concerts symphoniques de Montréal, the Montreal Symphony Orchestra, and the Toronto Symphony Orchestra. As a conductor, opportunities were less frequent, but her skill was nevertheless recognized, and she appeared numerous times with chamber orchestras and the CBC Symphony Orchestra of Montreal for broadcast productions. In 1946 Sir Ernest MacMillan invited her to be the first woman to conduct the Toronto Symphony Orchestra in a live performance at Massey Hall – then Canada's equivalent to Carnegie Hall.

The performance was memorable and the critics showered her with praise. Edward W. Wodson's column bore the title, "Woman's Hand Works Marvel for Orchestra: Ethel Stark leads Toronto Symphony to New Heights." Another wrote, "The orchestra played last night as if under a spell.… For downright glory, full-voiced brass and reed harmonies, the playing might have been Philadelphia's best in the Stokowski days." Gordon Ross claimed that her abilities were "impressive" and remarked that the Mendelssohn work she conducted "would have done credit to a [Sir Thomas] Beecham."[52] The war had depleted the TSO of important players, and the general consensus amongst the critics in Toronto was that the quality of playing had deteriorated because morale was low. It was indeed a great achievement for Ethel Stark to be credited with working marvels for the orchestra and more especially to be compared to the famous Leopold Stokowski, a legend in the conducting world, and by critics of a city that was in direct competition with Montreal.

The most touching moment, however, was at the end of the performance, when several women who had gained employment with the TSO during the war to replace the men serving overseas came up to Ethel and said, "Madame, we are so, so proud of you!" Ethel Stark had become a shining role model for many women.

"I am proud of *you*!" Ethel replied in return, and they all embraced.

Around this time, Fritz Reiner – the conductor who had once banned Ethel from his class because she was a woman – invited her to become the concertmaster of the Pittsburgh Symphony Orchestra, of which he was music director. This position of being second-in-command next to the conductor could have been another privileged "first" for Ethel and for women in the music profession; at the time there were no female concertmasters in major American orchestras. Ethel seriously considered this most prestigious offer. She had made her peace with Fritz Reiner many years ago and had heartfelt gratitude for all the opportunities he had given her. Should she go? The women's orchestra was a labor of love that brought Ethel very little money and not much recognition. There was the constant shuffling around from venue to venue. There were no major sponsors. And yet, there was warmth, commitment, and the knowledge that they were all doing something new, radical, and fun. After giving it much thought, Ethel Stark chose to "kiss goodbye" a steady financial future in America and stay in her beloved Montreal.

CHAPTER SEVEN
A Triumphant First

Despite the many ongoing challenges, the orchestra continued to attract members. By 1946, there were more than eighty players, and Ethel and Madge were determined to increase membership. Although the orchestra was improving at a rapid pace, it became quite clear that to prove their worth the women's orchestra needed a catalyst to propel it into the international scene. Only then would they gain the credibility they were striving for and deserved. Ethel and Madge could only hope that someone with a radical spirit would recognize the worth of the organization.

One night in 1946, Nicolas Koudriavtzeff, a manager for the American-Canadian Concerts and Artists Inc., invited a concert impresario who worked for Sol Hurok in New York City to attend a MWSO concert. Koudriavtzeff, who arranged international solo violin performances for Ethel, had attended several MWSO concerts before and had become a fan, but his friend, who had heard his share of "feminine" ensembles, was not particularly keen on sitting through an entire concert full of such spectacle. What could be so different about this Canadian women's symphony orchestra? He offered to stay for the first half of the program. So impressed was he after hearing the first two pieces that he decided not only to stay until the end of the concert, but also to offer the MWSO a serious and unprecedented musical opportunity.

When the concert ended, Ethel Stark walked off stage and headed straight for her dressing room. She was tired and didn't want to see anybody. Just as she was about to open the door, Koudriavtzeff and his colleague ran up to congratulate her.

"We would like to make you an offer," he said. "We want to take the orchestra with us to Carnegie Hall!"

Ethel let out a boisterous laugh. What a sense of humor this man had! Carnegie Hall, indeed. She murmured that it was a good joke and continued to her dressing room.

But the two gentlemen put out their arms to stop her. They reassured her they were serious.

By now Ethel was getting rather annoyed. "Gentlemen, please. I'm in no mood for jokes tonight. I am very tired."

"This is no joke, Miss Stark," insisted the impresario. "I am quite serious. I was pleasantly surprised and impressed with what I heard and saw here tonight. I think you and your orchestra would perform a fabulous concert center stage in New York." Ethel could not believe her ears. Plans were made to discuss the matter the following night.

Dinner at the Ritz-Carlton Hotel was marvelous, but even more amazing was that by the end of the night, Koudriavtzeff, the visiting impresario, Ethel, and Madge toasted their future trip to New York. The MWSO was going to Carnegie Hall.

♫

The following week, on Wednesday night, the women gathered for rehearsal. Business was as usual – a little bit of chitchat at the beginning, silence at the *tap, tap* of the baton, and playing of the repertoire, followed by the usual ten to fifteen minute break. But as the rehearsal was about to recommence after the break, Ethel stood on the podium, looked at the players, and announced non-chalantly as she passed her baton from one hand to the other, "I am planning a concert for you on the stage of Carnegie Hall."

A few giggles were heard. Others ignored the comment and continued adjusting their instruments.

"We'll take the train overnight and get there in the morning," continued Ethel. She went on to explain the logistics of the trip.

"We thought she was joking at first," Lyse Vézina recalls. "But when she said she was serious, we nearly dropped our instruments! Don't forget this was a women's symphony orchestra from Canada…nobody would have ever thought it would happen. Not even a Canadian male orchestra had played in Carnegie Hall!"

The offer to play in Carnegie Hall was indeed a tremendous one – the first in Canadian history. No Canadian orchestra had ever been invited to debut professionally in the US. Even established orchestras in Canada were vying for an opportunity to tour or perform on American soil in order to establish an international reputation. The Toronto Symphony Orchestra, for instance, had tried tirelessly to be invited by an American agency. Their offer did not come until 1951.

Here, then, was Ethel Stark, a female conductor, with the opportunity to have her women's orchestra be the first Canadian orchestra to debut on American soil, and not in any distant town and shabby little theater but in the most musically active city and the most important cultural venue in North America. Carnegie Hall represented the pinnacle of success in the music profession. Given the general indifference of Americans toward Canadian orchestras, the invitation from Sol Hurok's firm was nothing short of a miracle, the opportunity they had all been waiting for, and the reward for their years of hard work.

The women could hardly believe it. There was so much excitement that night that they barely got through the remainder of the rehearsal. Chitchat, whispers, and shuffling feet forced Ethel to tap her baton several times. It seemed that nobody could concentrate on the pieces. Lyse and Pearl Aronoff began to wonder how on earth Ethel had managed to arrange such an event. Helen Demuth and Sybil Shattner, both of whom had little previous performing experience, wondered what it would be like to play on the most prestigious concert stage in North America. Antoinette Carta, Ethel's young violin student, wondered if they were really up to the job. Violet Louise Grant was overjoyed. Playing in New York City's Carnegie Hall was the opportunity of a lifetime. She was imagining what it would be like to set foot on the stage when Ethel asked her to remain behind at the conclusion of the rehearsal. Violet Louise thought perhaps she had done something wrong during the practice.

After rehearsal, Violet Louise approached Miss Stark, who had a worried look on her face. "Do you know anyone in New York City?" Ethel asked her. "Do you have any family there?" Ethel was worried because she knew racism was still very much part of the American landscape and felt she had to take extra precautions in case people saw Violet Louise's skin color as a problem.

"She was worried the hotel might not let me stay there and I wouldn't have anywhere to go," Violet recalls, and with tongue in cheek adds, "Imagine getting there and not having your second clarinetist!" But Violet's older brother had been to New York City and later assured them that it was such a cosmopolitan place, such a mixed city, that there would be no major problems. Violet Louise would go to Carnegie Hall.

The months leading up to their American debut were filled with anticipation and excitement. There was so much work to be done. The contracting agency had agreed to pay for the costs of the hall and the performance itself, but the women would have to pay for their own hotel bills, as well as transportation and meals. Madge and Ethel presented their case to the government. The Province of Quebec granted them $1,500, while Montreal's mayor, Camillien Houde, offered them his patronage. Although these were welcomed aids, they were not enough to even cover the transportation costs.

Planning Carnegie Hall Concert

MRS. H. B. BOWEN, left, founder and president of the Montreal Women's Symphony Orchestra, with His Worship, MAYOR HOUDE, and MISS ETHEL STARK, violinist and permanent conductor of the orchestra, as they discussed plans for the forthcoming concert in Carnegie Hall, New York, to be given by the orchestra October 22nd. The programme will be given here prior to the Manhattan performance on October 15th at Plateau Hall.

Camillien Houde, the mayor of Montreal, offered his patronage to Madge (left) and Ethel in order to help raise funds for the orchestra's trip to New York.

More fundraising efforts and more pleas for financial aid met with some success, but a couple of months before the venture, excitement suddenly soured into profound disappointment as Madge, Ethel, and Doretta faced the news: Despite all their efforts there was still not enough money to go to New York. The concert would have to be cancelled.

Ethel sat disheartened in her studio, elbows on the table, scanning all the paperwork. How would she tell the musicians? How could she let them down? Doretta assured her they had done everything they could. There was simply not enough money. Just as Ethel was gathering the courage to face the grim reality, there was a knock on the door. Madge Bowen walked in looking rather flushed. She took off her hat and set an envelope on the kitchen table for Ethel to inspect.

"It is from an anonymous friend of our family," Madge said, and went on to explain how this "anonymous friend" had sold some of his farmland to help them realize their dreams of getting to Carnegie Hall.

"He was a loyal Canadian who had much sympathy for the women's mission," recalled Ethel years later, "especially since the government had refused to back us in this important project of international stature.... It was such a hefty sum of money." It touched her to know that someone out there believed in their fight for equality so strongly and had such a love for his country. "*Tzedakah*," Ethel thought as she folded the letter and placed it back in its envelope. The dream was going to become a reality. Now that the concert in Carnegie Hall was secured financially, their musical diligence had to increase.

♪

The week leading up to the MWSO's big American debut was frantic. Nerves escalated, tensions mounted, and tempers flew (and sometimes so did the sheet music) as frustration set in. One day they would be walking on clouds, happily humming their melodies, and the next they would be walking on eggshells. While it is true that music can bring people together, when an orchestra is composed of individuals of such diverse backgrounds, disagreements are bound to surface. And given all the excitement and the amount of organization required of such a major venture, it is no wonder that during one rehearsal, what began as a debate between two women soon turned into a squabble, with one woman losing her temper and the other immediately retaliating. It seemed as if they would lunge at each other at any second.

"The two of them almost got into a fight," recalled a cellist years later. "It was really something!" Clearly, emotions were running high.

But before chaos broke out, Ethel intervened and with one word – "Enough" – put it all to rest. She had no time for petty squabbles. Besides, she was the maestra and during rehearsals her authority was the law, regardless of the opinions and feelings of the musicians in the ranks. More importantly, they were here for the music and for a cause. They couldn't let small differences stand in the way.

This was the only major quarrel that erupted in the twenty-five years of the orchestra's life. And while there were disagreements now and then – especially given Ethel's strong character and iron will – the presumption that women were quarrelsome and ill-tempered and could therefore not work together in harmony was nothing more than a stereotype. Ethel later remarked,

> Had I subscribed, however, to the age-old axiom that women are spiteful and disloyal toward each other, I should have lost little time in refusing the task offered me, preferring to go along with the less-involved career of concert violinist. But I knew – and it remained for the women of the orchestra to bear me out – that a group of women banded together in common enthusiasm could be willingly regimented to the necessity that there must be a leader, and that the leader's orders must be law, both in rehearsal and performance. As conductor of the MWSO, I can give the lie to all clichés having to do with the rebellious female, at least insofar as music is concerned.[53]

For tonight, at the *tap, tap* of the baton, all players resumed their positions and the rehearsal continued. There was still much work to be done.

♫

As the big day drew closer and closer, the practices intensified and so did the pressure to practice harder than ever. The musical program was a difficult one, the hardest repertoire they had yet attempted. And although the vast majority of women put their hearts and souls into the preparation, not everyone was enthusiastic about putting in double the work. After all, they were not being paid to do this – in fact, they would have to pay for their own travel – and they had many duties at work and at home. How could they be expected to put in any additional time, even if for a good social and artistic cause?

At their last rehearsal before heading off to New York, just as Mildred gave the signal to the oboist that it was time to tune, the door flung open. Panting, one of the first violinists entered the hall, took off her mittens, rubbed her hands, and made her way through the maze of chairs to her seat in the violin section. She was one of the better violinists in the orchestra; in fact, she had various professional jobs. The orchestra benefited from her expertise – or so many of them thought, including this violinist. Just as she was unzipping her jacket and preparing to sit down with her instrument, Ethel hollered, "Don't bother taking off your coat; you're not coming with us."

"It was really something!" recalls Violet Louise. Ethel didn't even look up at the young woman. She just stood on the podium, holding her baton and calmly looking at the score. "The violinist had missed two rehearsals and thought she could just show up to the last one and come to New York. But Miss Stark wouldn't have it! Yes, she was a very good violinist, but this was beside the point."

Ethel pointed to the door and the woman had no choice but to gather her things and leave. There was too much at stake for the other women to let one member treat this as a trivial project. Ethel would rather work with devoted amateurs than uncommitted professionals.

As the door shut, Ethel took up her baton and the work began. For nearly an hour she was on her feet, shouting instructions, swearing under her breath, wielding her baton like a weapon, her arms outstretched, sweat pouring down her forehead. The determination on her face was obvious: her dark eyes penetrating, her dark hair swaying back and forth, the veins on her forehead pulsating. During the break, Doretta brought a soda to hydrate her. After fifteen minutes the rehearsal continued with more of the same cajoling as before. The musicians responded to their leader, and anyone who would have sat in on their session would have seen a group of dedicated artists meticulously working out the subtleties of the music. At last nine thirty came around and it was time to stop. In a few days, these suffragettes of the symphony orchestra would perform their first international concert, and in some small way, women everywhere would be able to partake in their triumph.

♫

On October 21, 1947, the members of the Montreal Women's Symphony Orchestra met at Windsor Station to catch the night train to New York City. Suitcases, instruments, equipment, pillows, purses, personal belongings, and more than eighty women crowded the platform, ready to board the train.[54] Kisses, handshakes, and good-byes were exchanged with relatives. The train doors shut and they were off to America. Every mile of the journey brought more excitement and expectation. Some women couldn't sleep, others wondered if they were awake or dreaming. Instruments shifted from side to side as the train went around curves and there was such a flurry of activity trying to hang on to them that even those women who had fallen asleep were momentarily awakened.

"It was quite something," recalls Lyse. "It was like that movie with Marilyn Monroe, *Some Like It Hot*, with all the female musicians. That's what we were: a pack of women hauling their instruments on the train. It was exciting! When we got there the next day we were all nervous and tired, but that's because we couldn't sleep on the train."

Members of the orchestra gathered at Windsor Station to board the overnight train to New York.

As the sun began to rise, those who were still awake knew they must be getting close. How lucky those women were who were still sleeping! Then at last bodies began to shift, arms stretch, and eyes open. The train came to a full stop at Grand Central Station – they had arrived in New York City.

"There were almost one hundred women getting off the train. There was so much excitement!" recalls one of the members.

The women scrambled to check in to the Wellington Hotel on Fifty-seventh Street, while Ethel, Doretta, and Madge went straight to the upscale Plaza Hotel on Fifth Avenue. After everyone had settled in and they had grabbed something to eat, Ethel rushed off to Helena Rubinstein, the famous cosmetician, for hair and make-up before the photo session and interviews for various newspapers. Although newspapers across Canada had publicized the event months in advance, emphasizing its significance, when it came time to cover it, only Thomas Archer, music critic of the *Montreal*

THE MONTREAL WOMEN'S SYMPHONY ORCHESTRA

led by its permanent conductor

ETHEL STARK

makes its *American Debut* in *New York*

WEDNESDAY EVE (8.30) OCT. 22 in **CARNEGIE HALL**

under the distinguished patronage of:

the Honourable Omer Coté, Secretary of the Province of Quebec.

His Worship the Mayor of Montreal, Camillien Houde.

• The first of the five major Canadian Symphony Orchestras ever to appear beyond the borders of Canada.

•80 women musicians

Past history : Seven full Canadian seasons from 1940 to 1947.

For year 1947 : Tour of United States and Canada Regular Montreal season.

For year 1948 : First European Tour:—Concerts in Great Britain, Holland, Belgium, France, Italy, Switzerland, Czechoslovakia, Norway, Denmark, Sweden.

Printed in Canada

Exclusive Management:
American-Canadian Concerts & Artists,
59 W. 55th Street, New York.

Gazette, made the journey. Much to everyone's disappointment, it didn't seem that Canada was all that interested in the women's revolutionary endeavors abroad. Fortunately, the American press thought the event quite newsworthy and sent some of its most noted reviewers to cover it.

Back at the Wellington Hotel, the women unpacked their belongings and practiced their instruments. Some of them tried to sneak in a nap. A few telegrams from friends, family, and fans were already waiting at the reception desk for bassoonist Helen Bacal; they were so proud of her.

"We all wish you good look and success in your New York Debut," wrote the Rubin family.

"Hope Carnegie roof does not cave in from ovation tonight. Good luck," wrote friends from the office where she worked.

"*Courage, Hélène, jouez bien et bonne chance,*" wrote another supporter.

Indeed, regardless of what objections families or friends may have had to the women playing in an orchestra, they couldn't help but be proud of such an achievement. This was no ordinary concert.

"We were very proud of Violet. We could talk of nothing else!" recalls Joyce Grant, Violet Louise's sister.

After pictures and interviews, Ethel hopped in a limousine and headed directly to Carnegie Hall, where she met up with the rest of the orchestra. Everyone was nervous and excited. Women paced up and down. Some blew quietly into their instruments. Some held each other's hands. Violet Louise and violinist Helen Demuth practiced their difficult passages one last time. Percussionist Violet Archer tried to visualize her performance. Bassoonist Esther Litman and French hornist Sybil Shattner cleaned their instruments for the tenth time. Another young cellist hoped elderly Marie Brazeau would be able to withstand all the excitement, while seasoned performer Gertrude Probyn hoped that young violinist Antoinette Carta would be able to handle the pressure.

Madge gazed at her orchestra as a mother looks at her children, with much pride and affection. Seven years earlier, people had said

Flyers promoted the Carnegie Hall concert.

they were crazy and that a woman's orchestra would never succeed. Seven years earlier, they had been practicing in their kitchens and living rooms, and now, here they were, about to perform at Carnegie Hall to a capacity audience of more than two thousand people.

It was now eight twenty-five, and Doretta, in her role as orchestra manager, announced that the players could take their seats on the stage. In a matter of minutes, America would be introduced to the Montreal Women's Symphony Orchestra. Alone in her dressing room Ethel wondered how the critics would react. Would the MWSO be able to do justice to Canadian artistic culture, or would they leave Americans with the impression that the arts in Canada were severely underdeveloped? The move to have a fledgling orchestra perform in one of the most important cultural venues in the world was indeed a daring one. Many members were nervous that they would not measure up artistically. Most of the women had only been performing for seven years and felt intimidated not only by the extensive education, experience, and success of the male performers who frequented the venue, but also by the importance of the event itself. They were the first Canadian orchestra in Carnegie Hall – the first Canadian orchestra to be invited to play in the United States – and would be representing the entire country. The elitism of the profession

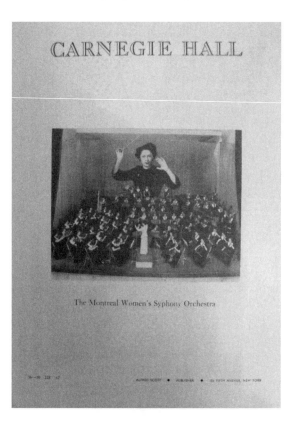

The Carnegie Hall program

itself also intimidated the many women who considered themselves regular working-class individuals, "office workers, factory
workers, and teachers."

Keeping all of their concerns in mind, as well as those in her
own heart, Ethel closed her eyes and began to recite the Twenty-
third Psalm, "The Lord is my shepherd, I shall not want. He leads
me beside still waters…. Goodness and mercy shall follow me all
the days of my life…"

Doretta knocked on the door to announce that the time had
come. Ethel could hardly believe it. This was the moment. This
was *their* moment. Knowing that her mother was in the audience
and that Lea Luboshutz, her violin professor at Curtis, had come
from Philadelphia for the occasion made Ethel feel a little more
confident. She took a deep breath and recited her prayer once
again.

At last, with some trepidation but a big smile, she walked onto
the stage. Applause greeted her as she approached the podium in
her glittering white gown tied with
a gold sash, her head held high.
The musicians leaped to their feet,
the string players rapped their
music stands with their bows,
and the woodwinds tucked their
instruments under their arms and
clapped. Ethel smiled, bowed her
head, and motioned the musicians
to take their seats. A palpable
silence fell. There was no noise,
not of breathing, nor keys click-
ing, nor feet shuffling. Eyes wide,
mouths half-opened, the women
looked at their conductor in awe
and reverence, as if they were
partaking in a solemn religious
service. Experienced professionals
like Mildred Goodman trembled
as if they had never been on stage

Elegant in her long white gown, Ethel
Stark acknowledged the applause from an
enthusiastic New York audience.

Earlier in the day of the performance the orchestra had a chance to rehearse at Carnegie Hall.

before; after all, there was a lot at stake. The baton almost slipped out of Ethel's sweaty palm, but she grabbed onto it and with a sudden sharp breath that cut the silence, raised it in an energetic upbeat, and the orchestra sprang onto the first rhythmic measures of Carl Maria Von Weber's *Euryanthe* Overture.

The music leapt and danced as the players swayed together as one, feeling every beat of the music. This was followed by the world premiere of Sir Ernest MacMillan's *Two Sketches based on French-Canadian Airs*, a piece written for this occasion, and Richard Strauss's Death and Transfiguration, op. 24 – a gargantuan work that even seasoned ensembles with long histories of performing on the world stage approach with caution. What could have compelled an orchestra of seven years to play this warhorse? Perhaps it was the chance to prove, once again, that they could do it, or perhaps it was to showcase the stars of the orchestra as talented and serious musicians.

The music soared, filling the prestigious facility, the place where the best musicians had performed: Sergei Rachmaninoff, Arturo Toscanini, Leonard Bernstein, and Arthur Rubenstein.

"It was such a big honor," says Lyse Vézina. "Carnegie Hall is the temple of music in America. It is still one of the best concert halls in the world. [After my time with the women's orchestra] I joined the Montreal Symphony Orchestra [and] I played in the best halls in the world...in Moscow, Leningrad, Vienna, Paris, London...[but] I would say Carnegie Hall was one of the most exciting experiences of my life because of how nervous we were trying to be up to the job."

"We couldn't believe it was happening," Violet Louise Grant recalled years later. "The place was so packed the night of the concert. It was really full. I didn't see any gaps, and there were so many levels and rows. It was such an experience.... [The orchestra] wasn't a high school band!" With that performance, Violet became the first black Canadian woman to play in a symphony orchestra at Carnegie Hall.

After a brief intermission the women went back on stage and gave an energetic performance of Tchaikovsky's challenging Fourth Symphony. "That's how good we were," Lyse recalls with excitement. "We played Tchaikovsky's Fourth, a very difficult piece. Imagine!…Yes, the orchestra was very good at the time. We were in top shape. It was the right moment for us."

Ethel confirmed, "We were at the highest point of our success."

If they began the concert overwhelmed and intimidated, after their professionalism kicked in nothing in the world mattered to them but the melodic outlines of the music, the rich harmonies, and the energetic rhythms. They simply loved to play. And they were here to *perform*.

Thunderous applause erupted from the audience as soon as the last trace of music dissipated. They shouted "Bravo!" and "Encore!" The concert had been an overwhelming success.

The critics approved. Olin Downes of the *New York Times* wrote, "Quietly, courageously, asking to be heard only on its merits, the Montreal Women's Symphony Orchestra, conducted by Ethel Stark, made its New York debut last night in Carnegie Hall. They play vigorously, rhythmically, and with a large measure of communicative fire."

Francis D. Perkins of the *New York Herald Tribune* said, "Its members are all proficient players of their various instruments. The individual players maintained a noteworthy standard. The performance was well balanced and well unified. The concert spoke well for the orchestra's spirit and vitality, as well as for its prevailing sonorities. Miss Stark's direction told of technical ability, authority, and knowledge of her scores."

In the opinion of Robert Bagar of the *New York World Telegram*, "The playing of this group was quite vigorous and, it goes without saying, quite delicate when that was necessary. In general, a praiseworthy exhibition by a most industrious energetic group of lady Orpheuses."

Harriett Johnson of the *New York Post* noted that "the adventuresome spirit of the feminine sex was demonstrated last night.… [I]t performed honestly with credible musicianship and an effective range of dynamics."

In *The New Yorker,* Robert Simon wrote, "Since we're well out of the era when symphonic playing or conducting by women was so infrequent that it had to be welcomed with generous allowances, the Montreal ladies may be considered simply on their merits as musicians. They're a good orchestra – the string section was fine, especially in Sir Ernest's charming sketches. The conductor of this orchestra is Ethel Stark, who directed with knowing musicianship and crisp, animated authority."

Another critic, Irving Kolodin, observed that the women of the MWSO "came out of the North, where men are men and women play trombones."[55] While there were many American women's orchestras, the majority employed men to fill in the low brass positions. The MWSO was likely the first full-fledged all-woman symphony orchestra to grace the stage at Carnegie Hall.

What an accomplishment. What a reward for all their hard work. Despite all the seemingly insurmountable obstacles, in only seven months the MWSO had performed their debut concert, and in only seven years they had made it to Carnegie Hall. Not only had this been an unprecedented opportunity that boosted the morale of the ensemble, but it also proved that its emphasis on women's teamwork and inclusiveness had paid off. The MWSO's performance in Carnegie Hall was a historical milestone for orchestras and musicians in Canada, and it was accomplished solely by the efforts of dedicated Canadian women. For many years, a portrait of Ethel Stark hung in Carnegie Hall to commemorate their achievement.

This lighthearted profile of Ethel appeared in the Oct. 4, 1947 edition of *New Liberty* magazine.

Woman of the Week
ETHEL STARK

FAVORITE AUTHOR
   I like Sinclair Lewis because he gives a musician like myself a down-to-earth picture of real life.

FAVORITE BOOK
   Goethe's Faust or Lin Yutang's Wisdom of Confucius.

FAVORITE MOVIE ACTOR
   Claude Rains

FAVORITE MOVIE ACTRESS
   Ingrid Bergman because she is an all-round artist and more than just a movie actress.

FAVORITE PLAYWRIGHT
   George Bernard Shaw or Eugene O'Neill.

FAVORITE PLAY
   School for Scandal or O'Neill's Mourning Becomes Electra.

PET HOBBY
   Sculpture, when I have time.

PET AVERSION
   ". . . the idiot who praises, with enthusiastic tone,
   All centuries but this, and every country but his own."
   (Koko in The Mikado)

FAVORITE COMPOSER
   Bach, Beethoven, Brahms (classical); Gershwin, if you consider him popular, otherwise Jerome Kern.

FAVORITE COMIC STRIP
   Li'l Abner.

FAVORITE ORCHESTRA
   It is hard for me to choose between the Boston Symphony, the Philadelphia Orchestra, and other fine American orchestras.

FAVORITE GRAMOPHONE RECORDS
   Recording of the Beethoven Eroica by Toscanini and Bruno Walter's recording of the Brahms Fourth Symphony. Also Sibelius' Second Symphony by Koussevitzky.

FAVORITE DRESS DESIGNER
   I am a devotee of Elizabeth Hawes' book, Fashion Is Spinach.

FAVORITE PART OF WEARING APPAREL
   My white-and-gold gown which I wear when I conduct the Montreal Women's Symphony Orchestra and which I designed myself. I enjoy wearing suits, not severely tailored, for afternoon wear.

FAVORITE SPORTS
   Golf and tennis (to play); ice skating (to watch).

FAVORITE SUMMER RESORT
   Carmel by the Sea, California.

WHERE I'D LIKE TO RETIRE TO
   A house in the country with my library of musical scores and my books.

FAVORITE RADIO PROGRAM
   Town Meeting of the Air.

FAVORITE RADIO STAR
   Fred Allen.

CHAPTER EIGHT
Growing Pains

In the years that followed their successful Carnegie Hall debut, the MWSO was on top of the world – or so it felt to the more than eighty women who had graced the stage. The musicians had gained such confidence that they dared to dream bigger and bigger. At last it seemed as if it would only be a matter of time before the orchestra evolved into a professional ensemble, receiving the recognition and the remuneration they justly deserved. Ethel and Madge now considered applying for financial support from the City of Montreal.

News of this woman's orchestra from Canada spread, garnering the MWSO even more national and international admirers. A London impresario offered Ethel Stark and the MWSO four concerts in London in July 1948,[56] while another leading impresario from Japan, Noboru Yoshida, offered them a tour of Japan and performances in major concert halls. Invitations came from England, Belgium, France, Holland, the USSR, countries in South America, and many other European countries.[57] After reading an account of the MWSO in a Japanese newspaper, a female fan enthusiastically wrote asking if it were really true that women could play instruments like the trombone. The MWSO was garnering so much international attention that Ethel and Madge couldn't wait to submit their funding requests to various government officials. They wanted a European tour, to expand their activities, and to have careers in the orchestra.

Opportunities were presenting themselves left and right, and while Ethel and Madge worked on gaining the attention of government officials, the MWSO set their sights on other Canadian cities, including Joliette, Quebec, and Windsor, London, Kingston, and Toronto, Ontario.

Their debut concert in Massey Hall, Toronto, was especially memorable. It was scheduled for April 12, 1948, but since Ethel and Madge had to arrive in Toronto the day before to greet the press and media, they decided to take the night train right after the orchestra's concert in Montreal on April 10. It was risky, but worth the try. Unfortunately, the concert ran late and it looked as if Ethel and Madge would miss their train. Doretta had been keeping a close eye on her wristwatch and had prepared for an "emergency" situation. When Ethel walked off the stage she was escorted to her dressing room where four members of the orchestra met her.

"One helped me out of my gown, another held my skirt in readiness for me to step into, another my blouse, my shoes, etc., until I was completely clad in my traveling outfit ready to leave," she recalled. But that was not all. Outside, a police officer on a motorcycle was ready to escort them to the station. What a sight it was – Ethel Stark and Madge Bowen driven in a vehicle led by a speeding police motorcycle, lights flashing, sirens blowing at stop signs. Despite the speed, they still got there fifteen minutes after the scheduled departure time. What would they do? They stepped off the vehicle and saw stewards motioning them to rush to the door. Doretta had telephoned the station and begged them to hold up the train. Madge and Ethel hopped on, the doors closed, and the train took off. It was such a mad rush that just as the doors slammed shut, Ethel realized she had forgotten her wallet. Doretta arrived early the following morning with Ethel's wallet in hand, just in time for the women to greet and meet the press.

At the time, a woman touring without a male companion or chaperone was frowned upon, but Ethel was rather unconventional.

Unmarried and self-supporting, she had traveled around the world, worked diligently to improve her career, made her own professional choices, and had no immediate plans to have children. The independence Ethel experienced in travel and in carving out her own career path was rewarding, but it was quite another matter for the women of the MWSO who were married and had children.

Massey Hall was Canada's Carnegie Hall in the 1940s.

Although most husbands took pride in their wives' achievements, not all were pleased that their mates were traveling around the country, tooting their horns or fiddling their bows while neglecting their duties at home, especially if they had young children. As for many women, childcare was a major issue for the orchestra members. Sometimes arrangements were made to leave the children in the care of the grandparents or an aunt, but if this was not possible, the husbands were now solely responsible for the care of their children. For some, this meant taking time off work. When men were the main breadwinners and their wives were touring not for an added income but strictly for enjoyment, this was especially problematic. Yet it seems that for the vast majority of the time the women managed to juggle rehearsals, work, and motherhood without disturbing their commitment to the orchestra. But

Ethel and Madge were greeted on the
station platform by Patsy Parr, a young
Toronto pianist.

on this particular occasion, childcare was such a major issue that some women arrived only an hour before the Toronto concert and didn't have the chance to attend the dress rehearsal. Ethel was not terribly pleased, but she understood the sacrifice these wives and mothers made just to be a part of the ensemble.

The Massey Hall performance that night was received warmly by the audience and with favorable reviews from the Toronto critics. Edward W. Woodson of *Music Notes* wrote, "It was sheer music of spontaneity," while Colin Sabiston of the *Globe and Mail* noted the "deep impression made by women's orchestra." Under the headline, "Women's symphony delight to audience," music critic Augustus Bridle commented, "From the white-haired dowagers to young blondes, they were 'en masse' when the conductress came on stage."

Their success brought more opportunities, including offers from the Canadian Broadcasting Corporation to perform on radio and television. This offered them the chance to reach new audiences as well as some financial compensation. Some live appearances were gratis, but most paid good sums of money. After all, playing as a violinist for radio broadcasts is how Ethel had supplemented her income throughout the 1930s. But there was also a great deal of risk in playing over the airwaves, and naturally, the musicians found performing in the studio to a large invisible audience particularly stressful.

"In those days nothing was pre-recorded and you had to be very good to perform on radio and television…. [T]he orchestra was very good at the time," recalls Lyse Vézina.

This kind of quasi-live programming was not for the faint of heart. Anything can happen, and in fact, many things did happen, from the funny to the nerve-racking. Lyse recalls that on one occasion the orchestra was already in Radio Canada's Studio 42, rehearsing the program, when suddenly a musician fell ill and simply could not perform. "Who could play on TV on such short notice?" says Lyse. What could they do? It was not an easy task to find a musician – a female musician for that matter – willing to take such a chance.

"Why not use a man and disguise him as a woman," someone

in the orchestra suggested, "with a black dress and a wig?" The orchestra members burst into laughter and applause – what a good solution!

Ethel laughed heartily but rejected the idea. It was much too risky and ludicrous. What if they were discovered? People would laugh. Besides, this was an all-woman orchestra and she was determined to keep it that way. Thankfully, Doretta managed to find a replacement and the player drove to the studio as fast as possible. The all-female performance went on as planned.[58]

While performing on radio and television had its challenges, it also brought Ethel and the orchestra a good deal of exposure, increased confidence, and some remuneration. Orchestra members were not paid a salary, but "we had some radio and TV appearances, and those paid, of course," explains cellist Pearl Aronoff. "We were professional musicians." The downside to this was that broadcasting rarely ever used the entire orchestra, and only those who participated in the broadcasts were financially compensated – usually just the string players. Ethel called this reduced chamber ensemble the Montreal Women's Symphony Orchestra Strings.

Nevertheless, the opportunity to play over the airwaves was a measure of triumph for an ensemble that had waged an uphill battle from the beginning. And, though broadcasting opportunities were few compared to what other Montreal ensembles were getting, the women appreciated the work. More importantly, audiences from across the country were introduced to this special orchestra. Listeners welcomed the debut broadcast. Madge Bowen later recalled that it resulted in multitudes of letters of admiration and appreciation.[59] Ethel recalled receiving more than one hundred letters from women across the country, wishing they too could be part of such an ensemble.

The media in Montreal noted all this national and international attention, and in the decade that followed, gendered references to the musicians as "grandmothers" and "lovely symphony sirens" gradually disappeared. Critics began to focus more and more on the technical and musical merits of the orchestra, as well as on Ethel Stark's interpretation of the repertoire. Though some critics and audiences were still not ready to consider the orchestra as "professional" and on par with other ensembles, they continued to note that the players were improving year after year. The orchestra's continued success marked the MWSO as one of the leading orchestras in Canada and Ethel Stark as one of the best rising conductors in the country.[60] Surely, thought Ethel and Madge, the City of Montreal had noticed their success and politicians would respond appropriately. They were ready to be rewarded as paid professionals and prepared applications for funding.

♫

With all the successes of the MWSO, Ethel Stark was also confronted with a serious decision concerning the orchestra personnel: Should they continue to accept any woman with the ability to "read a little bit of music," or should they now accept only semi-professional or professional players? It was a decision fraught with serious consequences and one that could very well decide the future of the organization. Madge wanted the ensemble to remain faithful to its roots and continue to accept any woman with a desire to play music, but she understood what was at stake and left the decision up to Ethel. After much consideration – especially taking into account all the international attention the orchestra received after its success at Carnegie Hall – Ethel decided to stop taking applications from amateur musicians and only accept semi-professional and professional women. This was the most practical decision for the organization, for it was no longer possible to teach women to play from scratch. The MWSO was now an orchestra of professional players. They had already proven to the skeptics that the women could play well. It was now about reaching the next level – to be paid as a professional ensemble. Could the women earn a living playing in the MWSO? She hoped so, but if this were to be the case, they would have to maintain a certain artistic level.

"The musicians that got in to play, they were already good on their instruments…it wasn't just anybody. They had to know their instruments well," Lyse recalls.

The orchestra became so good that besides attracting attention from fans around the world, it also attracted some of the best upcoming female musicians in North America, including Nathalie Clair.

♪

Nathalie Clair was born in Troy, New York, in 1922. She began double bass lessons as a young child with the encouragement of her father, who was a fine amateur flutist. Only a year after the war broke out, Nathalie won a scholarship to study at the Juilliard School of Music under Frederick Zimmerman.

One day in 1943, Erich Leinsdorf, who had recently been appointed director of the Cleveland Symphony Orchestra, attended a series of student recitals at the Juilliard School. Slim, dark-haired, twenty-year-old Nathalie walked onto the stage, set up her double bass, mounted her wooden stool, and began to play. It was uncommon for women to play large instruments – in fact, the larger the instrument the more scandal it created when played by a woman – and it must have been an unusual sight to see such a petite woman handling an instrument almost double her size. But stern-faced Erich Leinsdorf sat spellbound by the melodious and sonorous sound of Nathalie's contrabass. The more he heard, the more convinced he grew that he had found the perfect replacement for the empty double bass chair in his orchestra. The war was slowly reducing the membership in many orchestras across America. After the recital, he offered Nathalie the position.

It took Nathalie some minutes to realize that he was sincere. Would she leave Juilliard to join the Cleveland Symphony Orchestra? Nathalie smiled politely, and although her head and heart were racing, she remained composed. Leave her studies now? She was only halfway through her degree. Yet, the Cleveland Symphony Orchestra was considered one of the "Big Five" orchestras in the United States, and with the exception of the harpist who sat at the edge of the stage and who was only a part-time member, there were no women in the orchestra.[61] This was a rare opportunity and a great achievement. After much consideration, knowing that this is why she was attending the Juilliard School in the first place, she accepted.

In 1943 Nathalie became the first woman to be admitted as a regular member of the Cleveland Symphony Orchestra, and one of the first women to be admitted into a Big Five orchestra. She had a wonderful time playing with and learning from some of the best musicians in the country. After four seasons, she decided to take a break to get married and raise a family. Unfortunately, only a few years later, she became a widow.

Nathalie Clair-Feldman

In 1949, Nathalie moved to Montreal to start a new life. She found a network of support and sisterhood among the members of the Montreal Women's Symphony Orchestra, especially since many of them shared Nathalie's Jewish heritage. Ethel Stark was delighted to have this talented, experienced young woman join the group. Nathalie would provide strong support in the bass section, while the orchestra would provide her with a community of like-minded women. Nathalie's connection with the MWSO also proved to be useful in her personal life. Through Lotte (Goetzel) Brott's husband, she met her second husband and became Mrs. Nathalie Clair-Feldman.

Lyse recalls, "Nathalie Feldman was a virtuoso bassist. She was one of the greatest bass players I have ever known."

"She was an exceptionally gifted musician, but she was a woman," adds another member of the orchestra. "She could have gone very far…but she had a difficult time. She had to fight too."

♫

The MWSO was indeed succeeding in smashing gender stereotypes and in giving women opportunities to perform. It was also succeeding in a more important way: in instilling in the women a confidence that overflowed into other areas of their lives. This faith in their abilities not only manifested itself onstage during performances, but also offstage whenever they encountered any prejudice, sexism, or inequality.

Several years prior to her performance at Carnegie Hall, Violet Louise Grant had suffered a terrible act of discrimination that could have decided her future. She had finished high school among the top of her class, despite the fact that, as she says, "it was very difficult for black people back then.... I was the only black student in grade eight...most black students dropped out early on. I remember a child that dropped out in the seventh grade to work at a factory." But Violet succeeded and applied to the teaching program at Macdonald College (part of McGill University) and was accepted, much to her family's delight.

One day, however, Violet Louise discovered she had been ousted from the program. Certain that there had been a terrible mistake, she went to the administrative office to inquire about her situation. She was ushered into another office, somewhat perplexed as to why the secretary didn't simply correct the error. Why did she need to see the administrator?

After a few brief remarks, the administrator went straight to the point: Violet would not be able to complete a teaching degree because no white parents would want a black person to teach their children.

Violet Louise was dumbfounded. Again he repeated that no white parents would want their children to take orders from a black person. Oh, yes, it was true that many black Americans came here to study, but they would eventually have to go back to America to work. Her hope of becoming a black teacher in Montreal was futile, he said, and he refused Violet permission to continue in the program.

"I had some of the highest grades amongst my classmates, but that didn't matter," Violet recalled. "What was I going to do? We had little money." She worried so much that she became ill and was bedridden for some time.

This was potentially a life-altering moment. Violet could have

given in and chosen a different career path. But she determined that an act of prejudice and injustice would not be enough to keep her in the shadows.

Violet Louise Grant overcame prejudice and developed a successful career teaching her piano students.

And it was partly the experience of playing with the MWSO that drove her to slowly continue her pursuit of higher education.

When asked recently about the most important thing Ethel Stark and the MWSO had taught her, Violet Louise replied, "Confidence! Confidence in myself.... In my classes, I was invisible. Black people were made to feel as if they had no value [by society at large]." Within the orchestra she became an equal.

Violet Louise eventually completed a Licentiate of the National College of Music from the Quebec Conservatory of Music in 1952 and set up her own formal music studio. She had begun teaching piano lessons years earlier and now continued to expand her contingent of students – the majority from white families – and that number increased steadily over the years. Contrary to what the McGill administrator had predicted, no parent or child ever questioned her knowledge or expertise as a music teacher. She was so successful that her piano students were often featured in the newspaper.

As a performer, Violet Louise went on to audition for the mostly male Verdun Symphony Orchestra. She was accepted and performed concerts around the city, including at their home venue, the Verdun Community Centre – only a few blocks from her childhood home. Violet's talent as a clarinetist was also recognized by conductor Joseph Berljawsky, and in the late 1950s, he chose her to be a guest soloist with the Montreal Orchestral Society. All the while, she continued playing with the MWSO.

The women's orchestra had given Violet Louise more than a place to play music. In fact, with the validation she gained from years of playing with the orchestra, performing live in front of thousands of people, touring the country, being acknowledged as a performer by the public and as an equal by the other members of the orchestra, Violet Louise was able to go beyond the limitations that society placed on both blacks and women at that time. The orchestra's mission of inclusivity reinforced her confidence again and again. The orchestra was a vital part of her life.

♫

From the very beginning, Ethel and Madge had agreed that the orchestra must be inclusive of women of all backgrounds. This inclusivity turned out to be one of the most important benefits that the orchestra bestowed on its members. Ethel understood that sexism and racism are immutably connected. "My parents always instilled in me and my siblings in our formative years to respect all people regardless of color, creed, or race," she recalled. "At Curtis, I also met and befriended students from all around the world."

But one might wonder whether all the women of the MWSO shared Ethel and Madge's worldview. After all, Montreal was, literally, a divided city. The social lines were clearly stratified based on race, language, and religion. Indeed, the layout of the city itself reflected the division of ethnic backgrounds – west of Boulevard

Saint-Laurent was English, east of The Main was French. The lower-class communities were in between. Tensions caused by language differences escalated to such a degree that there was a time, from 1930 to 1942, when there were two city orchestras: The Montreal Orchestra catered to an English-speaking public and the Société des concerts symphoniques de Montréal to a French-speaking clientele.

Class tensions between various groups also intensified during the Second World War, and suspicion fell especially on the Jewish community. Canadian Jews, suspected of being Communists, suffered from employment discrimination, including the denial of welfare benefits and minimum wage, and from strict quotas set by businesses and institutions. Ethel too was the victim of discrimination. Her press secretary, James P. Komar, admitted she had suffered from anti-Semitism. "Of course she did.... Ethel was Jewish and proud of it; I admired her for that. And of course it impacted her [career] opportunities, especially in the anti-Semitic atmosphere which lingered for some time after World War II."

In one sense, the women's orchestra was also a reflection of the ethnic division of the city. Like the majority of the population in Montreal, more than half of the women in the orchestra were French-speaking and Roman Catholic, followed by a strong mix of English-speaking women of different Protestant faiths – Anglican and Lutheran – and women of Jewish heritage. Some English-speaking women were of other faiths, including Bahá'í. Orchestra rehearsals were held in English, despite the fact that most of the women spoke French. Both French- and English-speaking women had to take orders from a Jewish woman, and all of them had to work with each other despite society's widespread suspicion of those of different ethnicities. Women of the upper classes had to work with women of the lower classes. It must have been a humbling experience for an amateur socialite to compare herself with the younger maid who was progressing on her instrument at a faster pace.

When the orchestra first started, most men were overseas or otherwise involved in contributing to the war effort. Women were left to care for their children and their homes and were encouraged to aid the economy by working outside the home. Perhaps this made the creation of this diverse ensemble possible. The women of the MWSO were, for the most part, left to themselves to direct their private lives, which included the operation of the orchestra. However, when the war ended and their husbands returned home to resume their position as head of the family, women were expected to return to the private sphere. One MWSO musician recalls the situation of an orchestra member who was the wife of a wealthy upper-class businessman. She was an amateur who threw herself heart and soul into the ensemble. During the war her husband was away and she had plenty of time to help organize the orchestra's concerts. Her husband was initially pleased that his wife was doing something productive while he was away, but when he returned home full-time, he discovered just what kind of group the orchestra was – a mish-mash of women from various social classes headed by a proud and commanding Jewess. The husband was not at all happy to see his wife involved with such a rag-tag ensemble, especially not with Ethel Stark at the helm. Was her husband perhaps afraid of being called a Jewish/Communist sympathizer? Was he concerned that his wife's new friends would taint his reputation in the business world? Or did he simply dislike Ethel Stark and the other women? His wife showed such enthusiasm for playing in the orchestra that he grudgingly consented to her involvement, but would not attend the concerts. Indeed, there were other family members who did not attend the MWSO concerts either, although the majority of families were supportive of their women.

Unlike the society of the time, where animosity toward strangers was rampant, the orchestra became a safe place for the women who had come together to make music. While they belonged to different classes, they all had one thing in common – they were women, and as such, they all shared a symbolic second-class citizenship. They were all victims of prejudice in the music profession, in one way or another. Rather than constructing an identity tied to their ethnic, economic, religious, or linguistic background, they formed an identity based on their common goal: their desire to play music. Their involvement with the orchestra did not necessarily mean that they all embraced diversity in their daily lives – although some of them did. It did mean, however, that upon becoming members they agreed for those few hours a week to put all class divisions aside and let the orchestra be a neutral zone. As a result, social distinctions did not compromise the solidarity of the group, and the women were able to challenge the staunchly conservative system. Being part of the orchestra gave each woman the opportunity to work closely with those she may not have had contact with otherwise, and in a very intimate way, for music requires cooperation and trust. Within the orchestra, the women could relax and enjoy themselves, without worrying about the things that divided them. It was an environment where tolerance and mutual respect abounded. Within the orchestra, at least for those few hours a week, they all became equals.

Violet Archer, seen here composing, was a strong defender of human rights.

The MWSO mission extended to more than just the playing of music or even the breaking of barriers. As for Violet Louise Grant, it was about giving women the confidence to challenge prejudice in their daily lives or in the lives of other victims. Violet Archer, for instance, viewed herself as a loyal Canadian, but her vision of "Canadian" was one that embraced various peoples and cultures. She knew what it was like to be discriminated against because she was a woman, and she had befriended many Jewish women in the orchestra. As she read the reports of racial targeting of the Jewish community by anti-Semitic politician Maurice Duplessis during the Second World War, she became furious. One day, in a burst of anger she wrote a response to a letter in the *Montreal Star*, calling herself a "Gentile" who cared about human rights abuses.

Sir,

I would like to tell "Jewish Mother" that there are Gentiles who, on reading Mr. Duplessis's cruel attempt at Jew-baiting, were filled with real contempt for a politician who must try to use one of the basest of modern methods to gain favour with the working classes. I too have scanned the papers anxiously to see whether he would be put in his place – so far I have seen nothing of importance.

Obviously Mr. Duplessis carefully chooses his time for all his little tours de force. Well does he know how anxious we are not to confuse his train of thought with that of good loyal French-Canadians, who I am certain are as much against his most recent action as we are. You may rest assured, Jewish Mother, that there are Gentiles who care.

– Gentile[62]

As the years passed, artificial lines of class, religion, and language were slowly crossed and transcended. The members of the MWSO truly came together – and flourished – as an ensemble.

CHAPTER NINE
Decrescendo

The Montreal Women's Symphony Orchestra continued to expand its activities, playing regular concert series, presenting children's concerts, holding workshops for female students, and performing on radio and television broadcasts. On the surface, all seemed well. In fact, the situation looked very promising. All the while, however, the orchestra's foundation suffered blows that in the moment did not seem insurmountable but that in retrospect crippled the organization bit by bit.

The first setback came in 1950, when Madge Bowen, "the heart of the ensemble," became gravely ill. She was sixty-four years old and up to that point had no intentions of stopping her work with the orchestra. As a testament to her love and devotion to the ensemble, when it was clear that she would not survive, Madge conferred on her MWSO friend Dorothy Connell an important request: Would she take over the leadership of the orchestra and ensure its survival? Dorothy had been playing with the MWSO for a number of years and although she had doubts, she did not have the heart to deny the request of a dying woman. Not long after, on May 23, 1950, ten years after she co-founded the Montreal Women's Symphony Orchestra, Madge Bowen passed away. Her death was a shock to the women of the orchestra. A special concert featuring the music of Madge's favorite composer, Beethoven, was performed in her honor. That night, Madge's violin chair remained empty, with only the glimmer of the light of a white candle in memoriam of the "human dynamo" who had been the heart of their beloved orchestra.

"She was a woman of rare and beautiful character," Ethel wrote in her memoir. "She had a deep love for music and a tremendous admiration and respect for true artistry."

"Mrs. Bowen was a lovely woman," recalls Violet Louise Grant. "She welcomed everyone."

"Mrs. Bowen was the true founder," adds another member. "She was very important to the orchestra." Indeed, without Madge Bowen's energy and imagination, the MWSO would not have achieved nearly so much. Madge's financial resources, though ample, were not unlimited. Instead, she used her social status to establish associates, build rapport, and maintain confidence in the orchestra. As an upper-class woman and wife of a respected executive, she made the orchestra's mission more palatable to those who might otherwise hesitate to accept a group from such a mixed social background. The figure of Madge Bowen, what she represented, was almost as important to the orchestra's mission as Ethel's musical talent. Ethel, by the fact that she was Jewish in 1940s Montreal, could not have produced such an aura of esteem, despite her enormous talent. Moreover, Madge radiated all the good qualities of the orchestra to the outside world. While Ethel could be socially awkward, self-centered, and even rude, Madge was charming, well-mannered, and cheerful. If Ethel put her foot in her mouth, Madge would not only soften the blow, but also turn it into something positive. Where Ethel was brash, Madge was tactful. And where Madge was bashful, Ethel was bold. If Ethel dominated the spotlight, Madge worked quietly behind the scenes. It was a strange attraction of opposites that brought out the best in both women. They capitalized on each other's strengths and made up for each other's weaknesses for the benefit of the orchestra. "In all those years [of working together], we never had a disagreement," Ethel recalled. It was the combination of Ethel's iron will, energy, and outstanding talent together with Madge's social and financial expertise, unwavering commitment, and warm-hearted generosity that had propelled the ensemble all the way to Carnegie Hall.

Dorothy Connell tried for a number of years to honor Madge's request, but she was so busy running the entertainment for the Air Force and taking care of her children that she could not live up to her promise. Ethel Stark was the head and leader of the orchestra, but Madge had been its soul. No one could replace Madge Bowen.

Only a year later, in 1951, the health of Ethel's mother, Laura, took a turn for the worse and she had to be hospitalized. Ethel was very close to her mother and this had a profound impact on her.

"It was May," Ethel wrote in her memoir, "the sunshine and warmth we had all longed for had come at last, but its loveliness could bring neither joy nor comfort to me and my sister, Doretta. For days and nights that seemed at once endless and all too short, my sister and I had been keeping vigil at my mother's hospital bed where she hovered between life and death."

On May 13, 1951, Laura Stark too passed away. Now Ethel and Doretta were on their own. Their father had died years earlier and their brother and his family were living miles away in Florida. The two sisters, now in their forties, unmarried and with no children of their own, were left to console and lean on each other for the rest of their lives.

Those two crushing blows – the deaths of her mother and of the president of the orchestra – left Ethel exhausted and disheartened. No one could replace Madge, and no one could take the place of her mother. But there were also many other women who were aging and passing away, or leaving the orchestra because they simply could not play any longer. When cellist Marie Brazeau became so old and ill that she could no longer play with the ensemble, the women of the orchestra brought her food, medicine, and companionship. They could not simply let go of a single elderly woman with no family of her own. They were, after all, just like family. There were other women who were leaving too as they moved on in life, and very gradually the original personnel of the orchestra began to change.

Meanwhile, the MWSO continued with its regular concert series, as well as the occasional radio broadcast and television appearance. But as the years went on, there was another change in the air: After the Second World War, orchestras slowly and cautiously began to accept women. While there were many members of the MWSO who were content to simply play in an orchestra where there were no steady financial benefits, there were many others who wanted more than what the women's orchestra could offer. They were restless to take their own place in the bigger professional world of music, as full-time performers, concert artists, educators, and composers – a world they had fought to change. They no longer wanted to be solely members of a segregated women's orchestra. The MWSO as an exclusive all-woman ensemble was slowly becoming a visible sign of a problem of the past. Thus, encouraged and strengthened by the training and education they had received for almost a decade, many of its members turned their attention to the openings in other major orchestras in North America or to other artistic and educational opportunities where their careers could flourish financially and artistically.

American women who had trained with the MWSO were also scoring "firsts" for women in music in their own country. Flutist Doriot Anthony Dwyer made headlines in 1952 when she became the first woman to be hired as a principal player by the Boston Symphony Orchestra – one of the most conservative "stronghold" orchestras of its time. Trombonist Dorothy Ziegler also became a "first woman" when she was hired by the St. Louis Symphony Orchestra to play in its brass section. Women of the MWSO were slowly breaking into the male bastion of the symphony orchestra around the continent.

Encouraged by the civil rights movement led by Martin Luther King Jr. and by the emerging women's liberation movement, in the 1960s the American Federation of Musicians began to lobby for increased opportunities for female musicians in symphony orchestras. This resulted in even more doors opening for women in major orchestras. Excited by the opportunities available to them, members of the MWSO slowly but surely moved on to paying positions in professional orchestras to make full-time careers in music.

Watching members leave the orchestra brought mixed feelings to Ethel Stark, the women left behind, and the supporters of the MWSO. On the one hand, Ethel knew that the goal of the women's orchestra was being fulfilled: After gaining enough training and experience in her orchestra, women were moving on to professional careers in other, better paying organizations. This at least proved that social impediments to the performance of women on the orchestral stage had been based on unfounded prejudice. On the other hand, if this trend continued, the women's orchestra would instead be viewed as nothing more than a training ground for feeding the "professional" male ensembles. Bearing the stigma of the "training orchestra" was on par with being an undervalued "feminine" orchestra – that is, mostly recreational, social, and amateur. Furthermore, women's music-making would not be appreciated on its own merits but continue to be viewed in relation to that of men.

Unfortunately, the gaps in personnel were very difficult to fill, and this was exacerbated by Ethel's decision to take applications only from professional musicians. It was not easy to find professional female musicians who could play woodwind and brass instruments and would do so for free. Importing musicians from the United States was expensive because their transportation fees had to be covered, and there was little money.

"People [would] come and go," recalls Lyse. "Sometimes we lost members and Ethel had to hire people for the concerts. Vacant seats are hard to replace. How do you replace a timpani player? You don't find them easily.... Sometimes we would need a trombone or a tuba player and Doretta would call and hire people from the States to come and play in the concerts."

Lyse Vézina

"It was too difficult to keep the orchestra running," said a violinist who played with the orchestra. "Women wanted to be paid as professionals too. They wanted to join the major orchestras and lead successful careers. They had fought for them."

Besides, recalled a cellist, "The women were getting old… many of them were in their thirties or forties when it all started…. Ethel was also aging." Many of the founding members had indeed moved on with their lives.

In addition, the orchestra still had no rehearsal space of its own. For more than a decade the women moved around from their kitchens to basements, to empty stores, to church halls, to drafty lofts, to warehouses – wherever they were given permission to practice. "Sometimes it was a warehouse, sometimes somewhere else," said Lyse. "After some years we moved to Plateau Hall. We had some rehearsals there, but you had to pay [and] the orchestra had a small budget…. We were always looking for a place to rehearse."

The MWSO had a big problem on its hands, and it would only get worse with each passing year: Finances were drying up. The Bowen family had been one of the main supporters of the orchestra, and with Madge gone – and all the expertise she brought along with her – the ensemble's activities began to diminish. By the late 1950s the MWSO became akin to a family surviving on a month-to-month paycheck, always wondering what the next month would bring. It became clear to everyone in the orchestra that times were changing, and if the MWSO hoped to survive it would have to adapt to the modern world, perhaps by inviting men into the orchestra. That would surely catch the attention of the City of Montreal. But was Ethel Stark ready for such a move?

"Segregation was a very controversial thing at the time," shared Mary Terey-Smith, a contemporary of Ethel Stark. "Perhaps if Ethel hadn't been so adamant about having an all-woman orchestra it would have lasted longer. But she wanted it to be all women."

Ethel Stark was not at all inclined to make the Montreal Women's Symphony Orchestra an integrated ensemble with both sexes. She would persevere.

Then, the final blow fell. The applications the MWSO had

prepared for funding were rejected, one by one. The Canada Council denied them funding based on the claim that the orchestra was in the "wrong geographic location." No one ever explained to the MWSO what this meant. But as pianist Sonia Slatin later recalled, "This amazing rejection spelt the doom of the Women's Symphony."[63]

Without any major financial assistance, the MWSO could not hope to survive for long. Keeping a symphony orchestra in operation is an expensive venture to undertake, even when its members donate their services. The hundreds of expenses that arose from running the organization year after year soon accumulated a deficit that could not be covered by ticket sales and private donations. In addition, the MWSO's frugal revenue was simply not enough to allow it to expand its activities to the same level as the male orchestras, including increasing the number of concerts during each season and commissioning new works. All the international invitations they received to perform in Japan, England, Belgium, France, Holland, the USSR, countries in South America, and many other European countries, would have to be declined. More importantly, the MWSO would not be able to pay its members a salary. In fact, in the almost thirty years of the orchestra's existence, no one ever received any salary or pension – a rather fierce blow to those who remained single throughout their lives, unsupported by a spouse. Playing in the orchestra was largely a labor of love.

"We were all playing for nothing. Even after [some of us became] professionals," recalls Lyse. "We would always give Ethel our free time."

For the next few years an underlying suspicion about whose political interests the government was serving began to brew, until finally a journalist from Toronto broke the silence. In 1959, Hugh Thomson of the *Toronto Daily Star* observed that the women's orchestra had risen to such a degree of eminence that the male musical establishment, particularly the city orchestra (the Montreal Symphony Orchestra) felt threatened. In response, the City felt the need to defend it by ignoring the needs of the women's orchestra. In an article entitled "Montreal Snubs Women's Symphony," he noted:

It [the MWSO] might not be competing deliberately with the Montreal Symphony Orchestra, which has been rebuilt and greatly augmented by special grants, and has imported Igor Markevitch as permanent conductor; but the element of competition is there, because the Montreal Symphony [Orchestra] is still a rough-and-tumble ensemble of little personality and *esprit de corps*.... After 19 years of struggling, [Ethel Stark] has brought her orchestra to a professional status that is too hot and too close for comfort to the city symphony.[64]

A year later, after more rejections and more silence from what Ethel referred to as "big powers that be," Thomson again voiced his incredulity:

[The MWSO] is a unique orchestra that has had to struggle every inch of the way to attain artistic excellence; but now that it is no longer a rough, semi-professional ensemble, the city's bigwigs have cooled toward it and its director...now that it has passed the novelty stage and has attained professional status in opposition to the city symphony, Ethel Stark has been given to understand that she and her ladies "no longer have a geographical place in Montreal."[65]

It is telling that critics in the Montreal area did not take up pen and paper to defend the women's orchestra and that the MWSO's defenders came from Montreal's main economic and cultural competitor, Toronto. Thomson bluntly pointed out what many supporters of the MWSO had been suspecting all along: In the beginning Montreal had been fascinated and somewhat amused that this "charming" group of amateur lady-musicians was trying to invade a man's world – Montreal had swooned with pride when the orchestra came back from Carnegie Hall draped in glory – but once the women's orchestra ceased to be a novelty and had proven that it was far from a mere afternoon tea ensemble, it became a threat to the established order. A few years of life is what most cynics had predicted for the orchestra, but rather than declining in strength, the MWSO had only grown in talent, popularity, and vigor. Furthermore, it was almost an affront to the musical establishment that a "women's orchestra" had accomplished something no other Canadian orchestra had been able to do – perform successfully on American soil. How provocative it must have been to discover that these "lovely girls" with little or no music training had risen to such heights in only seven years. Is this why media coverage had been so paltry? Were they so unwilling to give women the glory they deserved? What if a male orchestra had performed this historic debut? Would this have changed things? These and other questions were whispered and discussed as suspicion grew.

To its supporters it seemed that the MWSO was being punished and systematically being swept under the carpet for not turning out to be the leisurely group originally predicted. Rather than remaining the amateur "feminine" orchestra of "girls, mothers, and grandmothers," the orchestra had achieved great things, and with a sliver of the resources allotted to male orchestras. The many female musicians who were now creating their own spaces within orchestras and music institutions all over North America were visible proof that this women's ensemble was no leisure-time activity. The MWSO itself now claimed a distinct space in the professional artistic life of Montreal, and indeed, of Canada.

The initial fears of the detractors over the potential threat of yet another orchestra in Montreal were coming true. The MWSO had been left unmonitored for many years and now wanted a part of the small pool of funding available to arts organizations. Any kind of funding awarded to the women's group would cut into the city's limited resources. To make matters more complicated, the Montreal Orchestra (which largely consisted of male members) had been rebuilt with special grants that "allowed the employment of more fine musicians and the extension of the concert season."[66] Author Frances Rooney, who interviewed Ethel in 1979, observed, "This rebuilt orchestra was to be Montreal's pride.... It was as yet too fragile to tolerate any competition real or potential. The simple existence of the Women's Symphony constituted threat."[67]

Sacrificed to reasons of the common good of the city, the needs of the MWSO were eclipsed by those of the veteran male performers who flooded back into the city orchestra in the postwar period. The city of Montreal poured its resources into rebuilding the male-dominated city orchestra to the neglect of the MWSO.

The MWSO members themselves had mixed feelings about this situation. Cellist Pearl Aronoff, who was by now one of the few female members of the city orchestra, explained that there was no real competition between the two groups, only perceived. The women's orchestra gave several concerts a season, but nothing in comparison to the busy concert schedule offered by the city orchestra. Clarinetist Violet Louise Grant States mused years later, "It wasn't really a case of competition…we were doing something different." On the other hand, percussionist Violet Archer later reminisced, "We became a really good orchestra. In fact, the male orchestra regarded us as a competitor."[68] Another female violinist said many years later, "We were a threat because we were women…. I question why did Ethel not try [building a women's orchestra] in a larger center."

The neglect by the establishment led Toronto music critic, the *Globe and Mail*'s John Kraglund, to wonder if the main problem with the MWSO was really one of "social relations" with the Montreal Symphony Orchestra, for although Ethel Stark lived in Montreal for most of her life and conducted orchestras around the world, the Montreal Symphony Orchestra never invited her to conduct one of its public concerts. She was sometimes invited to conduct the orchestra in radio broadcasts, but this was behind the scenes, with no limelight. And, as the husband of an MWSO cellist later remarked, "Ethel Stark was a figure of authority and confidence. There were few women conductors at the time. Men [musicians] had a lot of contempt for her. I don't think too many of them liked her for what she was doing." An MWSO violinist also remarked, "The orchestra is the instrument of the conductor. It was just such an anomaly for women to be conductors, to be in orchestras. Ethel lived in the wrong time period. She was too far ahead of her time." In her private papers, Ethel wrote, "I gave a good part of my life to correct something, and now I feel as if that work has not been appreciated."[69]

In retrospect, what was missing in all of these discussions about funding and competition was that the MWSO was not curtailing the number of professional musicians in the city but rather adding to the cultural life of Montreal. The MWSO women did not destroy the walls of the symphony orchestra; rather, they expanded its boundaries to be more inclusive. They did not set out to annihilate the established symphonic tradition; rather, they carved fresh traces in the sand to make way for new trends. They were working to modernize the symphony orchestra in the same way that other groups of men and women in Quebec were working to urbanize the province, to *faire du rattrapage* or "catch up" with the needs of modern society. It was in this milieu, amidst the many changes taking place in Quebec society, that the women of the Montreal Women's Symphony Orchestra prepared for the end.

CHAPTER TEN
Curtain Call

The problems that had seemed small in the beginning, mere challenges to overcome, had snowballed. Ironically, the orchestra's success in the development of female musical talent and the breaking down of gender barriers actually contributed to its own demise, as its members began receiving offers from first-class orchestras all over North America. And with no public funding, due to the threat the MWSO posed the city orchestra as a result of its high quality playing, Ethel Stark and the orchestra found itself in an untenable position. In addition, Madge Bowen was gone, many women were aging, new personnel was difficult to find, and money was running out. This confluence of obstacles finally brought the MWSO to its knees. The future of the orchestra was now not only questionable, but its life was sure to come to an end in the near future. The MWSO's concert schedule became more and more sporadic.

On December 11, 1965, the MWSO performed its final concert as a full orchestra of strings, woodwinds, brass, and percussion. The concert featured the music of Handel, Mozart, and Beethoven. No one had anticipated that this would be the last concert the MWSO would give as a full ensemble, but the lack of money and personnel made it too difficult to continue with the season. The fact that no living member remembers the last concert in great detail is a sign that, by this time, the orchestra was no longer needed. "Ethel called me and asked me to play for this concert," recalls a violinist. "She needed string players. It was the last concert the women's orchestra gave but we didn't know it at the time.... [Besides] we were so busy playing with other orchestras that I really can't recall it."

"I don't remember the last concert in much detail," echoes another. "I was already playing with the Montreal Orchestra, touring.... It [the women's orchestra] just sort of dissolved."

"We waited for Ethel to call us back for another concert, but she didn't. It was sad, but we knew the orchestra had served its purpose. Its mission had been accomplished," adds a cellist.

After twenty-five years, the Montreal Women's Symphony Orchestra gave its last concert almost unnoticed and almost forgotten. The general feeling was that the orchestra had accomplished its mission, and it had done so very well. But if Ethel had originally intended the orchestra to be a training ground for women, she certainly did not envision that it would disband before it had the chance to offer women paid careers. Thus, Ethel refused to put down her baton and instead decided to continue to work occasionally over the next few years with the orchestra's string section, the Montreal Women's Symphony Orchestra Strings.

♫

On April 4, 1968, the Montreal Women's Symphony Orchestra Strings arrived at the campus of Loyola College, Montreal, to rehearse for a concert that evening. When Ethel arrived, she could tell right away that the women were upset about something. She pulled the concertmistress aside to ask what was the matter. Mildred Goodman just looked at the floor. "What is it, Mildred? What's wrong?" Ethel asked. Mildred could barely get her words out. At last she whispered, "There are swastikas pinned up all over the drama room!"

Ethel rushed to the drama room. On the walls were painted

a multitude of giant swastikas, the emblem of Nazi Germany, anti-Semitism, and the horrors of the Holocaust. Ethel recalled the day one of her relatives had barely avoided being sent back to Germany to be executed in the gas chamber and the sad fate of his wife, child, and father. It made her both ill and furious.

Everyone had seen what a roaring lioness Ethel could be during rehearsals, but no one had ever seen her so irate. Her eyes glowed with fire. She clenched her fists and said, "I want those signs removed immediately!"

"I cannot do that," replied the superintendent of the building.

"Those signs must be removed before we come back this evening."

"I will not do that. I have no permission to take anything down from the room."

For a moment no one breathed as the two stood in a face-off in the middle of the room.

"Very well then. We will come back tonight. We will go onstage, but I will not lift my baton to conduct the orchestra. Instead, I will tell the audience why everyone is onstage, instruments in hand, and why no one is making any music."

"Miss Stark, please. The drama professor is gone for the weekend and won't return until Monday morning. I can't do anything about it."

"Call him then. Or tonight we will show up but will not play, and everyone will know why."

And with that Ethel stormed out of the room. Doretta rushed after her, but the other members of the orchestra, many of whom were of Jewish ancestry, just stared in amazement.

Back at home, Ethel tried to focus on the concert, but as she studied her score, she couldn't help thinking of a particular personal encounter with anti-Semitism. After the MWSO's concert in Carnegie Hall, Ethel had traveled overseas to give solo violin performances all over Europe, with Sonia as her pianist and Doretta as her manager. The women had planned to take a week of rest at a spa called Hofgastein in the Austrian Alps, but the peace and calm they hoped for was not forthcoming. The manager referred to one of their kinsmen as "a filthy Jew," the waiter tried to swindle extra money out of them when he discovered they were Jewish, the hairdresser bragged of being one of the Nazis' Storm Troopers, and the women discovered that the lovely tea garden had once been a way-station from which Jewish men, women, and children were rounded up like cattle and sent off to concentration camps. They packed their bags, refusing to support a place where anti-Semitism remained so strong.

When the MSWO musicians arrived back at Loyola College that evening, the swastikas had all been removed. The concert would go on as planned.

As the music soared, Ethel began to think back to the life of the orchestra. There had been so many struggles! But didn't justice come at a price? Didn't the hope of equality make the struggle worthwhile? As she stood on the stage leading these women in producing beautiful music, she thought of other pioneers who were working to end injustices. Just last night, on a stage in Memphis, Tennessee, the fearless civil rights activist Dr. Martin Luther King Jr. had claimed, "When we allow freedom to ring, when we let it ring from every village and every hamlet, from every state and every city, we will be able to speed up that day when all of God's children, black men and white men, Jews and Gentiles, Protestants and Catholics, will be able to join hands and sing in the words of the old Negro spiritual, 'Free at last! Free at last! Thank God Almighty, we are free at last!'"

Isn't that what the women's orchestra had promoted all along? That different groups of people, Jewish or Gentile, Catholic or Protestant, white or black, rich or poor, could collaborate? Hadn't the thrill and joy of playing music brought them together week after week, through snowstorms and blizzards, moving from one part of the city to another, hauling instruments along trams and buses, playing in rat-infested basements, warehouses, and the CPR cafeteria? How different the women were from each other and yet how common was their love of making music. Playing music together, helping each other learn to play instruments, suffering as sisters through jibes from the cynics, and conquering the formidable obstacles that had dissuaded them many times simply because they were women had strengthened their common humanity and dignity.

Before she knew it, the last piece had come to a close. But no sooner had Ethel put her baton down in her dressing room, when a page boy, agitated and panting, came rushing toward her exclaiming: "Dr. Martin Luther King is dead! He was shot a few minutes ago!"

All this was too much to bear. The swastikas in the dressing room, prejudice, racism, and now Dr. King assassinated! Ethel crumbled to the floor, placed her hand on her face, and burst into tears. She wept bitterly for a long, long time.

But as she wept, Ethel realized that the women of the MWSO had also been part of this great movement in human history. They were part of the women's movement and of the civil rights movement that opened up the door of opportunity and equality to women across North America. The MWSO had set an example of sisterhood and hope. In the footsteps of Dr. King, they had also shown the world that women, regardless of color, class, or creed, were capable of working together. They had all gathered together, year after year, without ever being paid a salary or pension, to make music and create hope.

Ethel thought of all the women who had trained in the MWSO and had won positions in prestigious orchestras across North America. She recalled clarinetist Violet Louise Grant, who had been denied entrance into the teaching program because she was black, and just last year had finally gained her two bachelor degrees from McGill University. What struggles she had encountered, and she had not given up. Ethel recalled percussionist and composer Violet Archer, who had finally found a job teaching at the University of Alberta. She recalled the American women, such as Sonia Slatin, who had jumped at the chance to play in a symphony orchestra, had traveled great distances for the opportunity to make a difference, and were now renowned soloists and teachers in their own right. She recalled the underprivileged women and the wealthy women, the professionals and the amateurs, who despite all their differences worked for a common goal. The MWSO had indeed smashed gender, racial, and class barriers.

As Ethel assessed the past, she was suddenly filled with great hope for the future. The days of the orchestra were now surely over, but the doors of opportunity were finally flung open to women of talent everywhere, and this had started in part thanks to the pioneers of the Montreal Women's Symphony Orchestra.

CHAPTER ELEVEN
Legacy

Although the orchestra officially disbanded after almost thirty years, its mission was vindicated. The Montreal Women's Symphony Orchestra played an important role in launching the careers of women across North America as players in symphony orchestras, music professors, public and private music teachers, authors, composers, and most importantly, as a group of role models to future generations of women. But the orchestra did more than just help the cause of women in music – it also contributed to the flourishing of culture in Canada, by both the repertoire and the soloists it supported and introduced to audiences in Montreal.

Music of the European canon represented two-thirds of the orchestra's repertoire, yet the orchestra made it its goal to introduce contemporary works of music, as well as those by American and Canadian composers and rarely heard composers of the past. In 1942, the MWSO gave the Canadian premiere of Herbert Haufrecht's *Ferdinand the Bull*. In 1954, it performed the Canadian premiere of Arnold Schoenberg's *Verklärte Nacht*, op. 4, during a rare program that also included Carl Friedrich Abel's *Symphony in E-flat*, Karl Ditter Von Dittersdorf's Concerto for Double Bass in E Major with Nathalie Clair Feldman as the soloist, and Schubert's

Mass in G Minor, No. 2, for Chorus and Orchestra. Two years later, it gave the Canadian premiere of Ernest Bloch's Concerto Grosso for String Orchestra, No. 2. The orchestra also gave other contemporary composers a platform for their works. In 1946, the MWSO premiered Violet Archer's "Sea Drift for Chorus and Orchestra." It also performed a part of Archer's *Tone Poem: Leaves of Grass* in 1942, Ernest MacMillan's *Two Sketches Based on French-Canadian Airs* in 1947, and Aaron Bodenhorn's *Fantasy for Solo Oboe and Orchestra* in 1951. Other contemporary composers included Percy Grainger, Paul Hindemith, Ralph Vaughan Williams, and Frederic Pelletier. Rare gems by rarely heard composers, such as Evaristo Felice Dall'Abaco and Carlo Giuseppe Toeschi, were also part of the repertoire. Maurice Ravel's *Piano Concerto for the Left Hand* was performed with the Austrian soloist for whom the work was written, Paul Wittgenstein. The audacity of the MWSO's repertoire is indeed astounding, especially when one considers the orchestra's frugal budget. Likewise, the roster of soloists is equally impressive – cellist Zara Nelsova, violinist Lea Luboshutz, pianist Sylvia Zaremba, and pianist, conductor, and opera commentator Boris Goldovsky, among others.

The experience gained from playing with the orchestra was also very important to those women seeking professional careers in music. Many women who trained with the MWSO did indeed go on to win positions in professional orchestras in Canada (Montreal, Toronto, Halifax, and Vancouver) and in the US (including Boston and New York). Some of them became private music instructors, conservatory teachers, or members of music faculties in universities and colleges. Dedicated and talented players such as Mildred Goodman, Lyse Vézina, Pearl Aronoff, and Marthe Iosch trained with the MWSO and eventually moved on to professional full-time careers with other ensembles in Montreal, including the Montreal Symphony Orchestra.[70] Vézina wrote a book about the Montreal Symphony Orchestra and her experience of being one of the first women in its ranks. Nathalie Clair-Feldman joined the McGill Chamber Orchestra, the CBC Radio Orchestra, and also won a position in the Montreal Symphony Orchestra, alongside MWSO alumni Mildred Goodman, Vézina, and Aronoff. In

1958, Nathalie became the principal double bass of the Montreal Symphony Orchestra. She passed away suddenly in Montreal on April 5, 1966, at the age of forty-four, leaving behind her husband and two little girls, Anna and Judith. McGill University set up a scholarship in memory of her remarkable talent.

In 1993, during an interview in celebration of her eightieth birthday, acclaimed Canadian composer Violet Archer recalled, "I was drawn into the orchestra to play percussion...so I played the drum, the cymbals, and glockenspiel...all the extras."[71] She played with the MWSO for eight years, contributing her talent and learning from the experience before leaving in 1948 to further her studies at Yale University. In 1961, the University of Alberta hired her as a music professor. Her musical talent was soon recognized and she went on to become the chair of the Theory and Composition Department. In 1983, she was made a Member of the Order of Canada. For her contributions to the musical life of Canada, the library at the Canadian Music Centre, Prairie Region, was named the Violet Archer Library in 1987. The breadth of the musical language of this great Canadian composer is also acknowledged in the name of the Canadian indie rock band, The Violet Archers.

Violet had a deep respect and gratitude for all the work Ethel Stark did for women in music. In 1946 she wrote a sonata for violin and piano and dedicated it to Ethel Stark. It is a work filled with Hebraic lyricism to honor Ethel's Jewish heritage. Together, they premiered it on CBC radio.

Violet never forgot how beneficial her years were with the Montreal Women's Symphony Orchestra. In a letter sent to Ethel in 1996, she wrote: "Being in that orchestra was a great learning experience in the 'inside' of orchestral sound, and it also made me conscious of the importance of the dynamic value of percussion instruments in the orchestral fabric."[72]

May Fluhmann, the cellist and timpani player and founding member of the MWSO, continued to play music with the women's orchestra until the end. She developed an interest in photography, bird watching, and writing. After becoming interested in Arctic exploration, she conducted her own research on polar expeditions and in 1976 published the book *Second-in-Command: A Biography of Captain Francis Crozier.*

Harriet Peacock was an American flute player who trained with the MWSO. She went on to become a private flute teacher, a composer, and the author of books on the flute.

Oboist Lois Wann, a close friend of Ethel Stark, was another American woman who played with the orchestra in the rank-and-file and as soloist on several occasions. She became one of the most sought after musicians in New York City and a professor of oboe at the Juilliard School of Music.

Natalie Hollern was an African-American oboist and English horn player who was a part-time member of the MWSO. She became a member of the National Symphony Orchestra in Washington, DC, and one of the most sought after English horn players in America.

Betty Barry was an exceptional trombonist who played in a brass quartet for the prominent agency, the Redpath Lyceum Bureau. She was constantly looking for more "serious gigs" and this eventually led her to join the MWSO. The MWSO gave her the opportunity to play all the "big" music of the symphonic repertoire.

New York pianist Sonia Slatin, Ethel's long-time friend, not only performed regularly with the MWSO, traveling back and forth from New York every now and then over the course of twenty-five years, but also acted as the orchestra's New York agent, securing discounts at Jewish music stores and making connections with other aspiring female musicians who would be interested in training with and contributing to the women's orchestra. Sonia earned a PhD in music and went on to become a professor of ear training and music history at Columbia University. She remained close friends with Ethel and Doretta Stark until her death in 2007.

Cellist Raymonde Martin came from a musical family in Montreal. She was a founding member of the MWSO and played there until 1950, when she won a scholarship to the Paris Conservatory of Music. She became a professor of music at the University of Ottawa in 1967.

The confidence Violet Louise Grant gained with the MWSO

eventually gave her the courage she needed to reapply to teacher's college years later, when she was almost forty years old. Thanks in part

Violet Grant States treasures her MWSO memories.

to the influence of American black civil rights activism, she was able to re-enroll at McGill University, where she completed a BA and BEd in 1968. She eventually became a public school music teacher and taught more than one thousand students a week. Over the years she has received many honors for her contributions to the community, including being named "Grande Verdunoise." With her brother, she is currently working to have the contributions of black Canadian railroad workers recognized. She has also set up scholarship funds for students at her previous elementary school. History books usually credit the beginnings of the end of segregation in North American symphony orchestras to the late 1960s.[73] But the end of segregation had begun much earlier, in 1943, when Violet Louise Grant joined the MWSO and became the first black person in a Canadian symphony orchestra.

At age eighty-seven, Violet Louise said, "Ethel Stark encouraged me to be who I am today. I can do things and I don't have to worry about people putting me down anymore. Being able to play in that orchestra was, I would say, the highlight of my life."

Doretta Stark was an independent piano teacher, oboist, music manager, and a best friend to her sister Ethel. Throughout their lives, Doretta remained the person Ethel could trust unconditionally, the person she could turn to for anything and everything, and the person who accepted her and understood her in a unique way. From the moment Ethel was born, Doretta was absolutely devoted to her sister's well-being. Right up until her death, Doretta shared and lived vicariously through her sister's life and work. She was one of the greatest gifts in Ethel's life. Only a few people fully understood how important Doretta had been to Ethel's life and career, so invisible did she make herself in trying to shine the spotlight on her beloved sister. One of them was Shepard Broad, the orphan that Adolph Stark had rescued from being deported back to Russia in 1920. In reference to a 1979 article written about Ethel, he wrote to her and said, "Had I written the article, there would have been at least one or two paragraphs about Doretta, your business manager and your right hand, but for whom some of what you have accomplished might perhaps been more difficult to attain, perhaps, unattainable."[74]

Doretta passed away on Ethel's seventy-third birthday, August 25, 1983, in the service of her sister. Ethel dedicated her unpublished memoir, "To my beloved sister, without whom I could not have accomplished any of these things."

Although this book only chronicles the activities of Ethel Stark as a conductor of the women's orchestra, she was also involved in a variety of musical activities and adventures too numerous to detail here. She was one of the most important violinists in the country, a musicologist, a university professor, a choir director, a music instructor, and a benefactor. As a solo violinist and conductor, she toured throughout many countries in Europe and Asia, including Switzerland, where she met and befriended composer Ernest Bloch. She was the first woman to conduct the Miami Symphony Orchestra (1957) and orchestras in Israel (1952, 1962) and Japan (1960). In 1952, she built a choir of forty voices from scratch in much the same way she had done with the MWSO and took it to

Israel for the First Annual Israel Festival of Song. After the MWSO and the MWSO Strings dissolved, Ethel started a mixed orchestra of men and women. By this time she was almost sixty years old and was also planning to start an international music festival in Montreal. For all her achievements, she was presented to royalty, including Queen Elizabeth II and the Japanese Imperial Family, and was recognized by the Canadian government for her role as an effective cultural ambassador for Canada and Canadian culture.

The MWSO had caught the attention and imagination of people from around the world, and as a result Ethel Stark became a "representative" of women in music and the face of the MWSO. Throughout the rest of her life, she was primarily acknowledged as the "woman conductor" of the Montreal Women's Symphony Orchestra. This both pleased and haunted her, especially later in her life when she wished others to know she had been much more than just the conductor of a women's ensemble. When she was ninety years old she ran into a friend who said to her, "I remember your violin playing over the CBC radio in the 1940s. It was incredible. Oh, what a beautiful tone!"

Ethel teared up because she thought no one remembered her days as a violinist. Nevertheless, the opportunities and attention she received were inspired not by who she was but primarily by what she did – that is, build an orchestra of amateur women musicians from scratch, lead its first public performance within seven months, and in seven years take it to Carnegie Hall. Largely due to her work with the MWSO, Ethel became the first Canadian woman to gain international renown as a female conductor, joining the ranks of trailblazers such as American Antonia Brico and Ethel Leginska from Great Britain.

Ethel Stark as she waited to meet Queen Elizabeth II.

Ethel was greeted by Prime
Minister Pierre Trudeau at a
reception after her appointment
to the Order of Canada in 1979.

Through her involvement with the
MWSO, Ethel opened doors of equal
opportunity for marginalized groups,
promoted the image of Canada as a land
of rich cultural resources, and inspired peoples the world over to
recognize the sheer potential of both Canadians and women. The
legacy of social justice Ethel inherited from her Jewish upbringing
ultimately provided her with the ability to inspire the women and
to galvanize their efforts to work for sweeping changes in the field
of music. Although she traveled as one person, she embodied the
entire entourage of MWSO women wherever she went.

For these and her many other outstanding contributions to
Canadian cultural life, she was appointed a Member of the Order
of Canada in 1979, received the Canada 125 medal in 1992, and
was elevated to the Order of Quebec in 2003. On May 9, 1976,
the Concert Society of the Jewish Peoples' Schools and Peretz
Schools of Montreal awarded her their annual prize for her contributions to Canadian artistic life. In 1980, Concordia University
conferred upon her the degree of Doctor of Laws *honoris causa* for

Lieutenant Governor of Quebec Lise
Thibeault made Ethel a Grande officière
de l'Ordre national du Québec in 2003.

her enrichment of the cultural life in Canada. She was also elected a fellow of the Royal Society of Arts in England. In 2011, Ethel became the oldest living conductor in the world at the age of 100. Queen Elizabeth II sent her a greeting card to mark the occasion. Ethel Stark and her work with the MWSO have been featured in numerous magazines, including *Time* and *Fashion*, and in two films by the National Film Board of Canada.

Although Ethel had many interested suitors and received several marriage proposals, she was not the type of woman who would give up her career to stay at home to raise a family. Following the death of her wartime sweetheart, she hoped she would meet someone who could accept her busy traveling lifestyle. Unfortunately, she never did. Her biggest regret later in life was that she never had children, but she was also at peace with the decisions she had made to pursue a career as a musician and conductor. In 1990, however, she was heartbroken by the theft of her eighteenth-century violin; she never played violin again.

Ethel passed away on February 16, 2012, at the amazing age of 101. As a true testament to her iron will, right up to her death she still lived on her own, walked to the supermarket to purchase her own groceries, and took public transportation to "see what's going on in the city." She is buried beside her dear and faithful sister in Montreal at the Spanish-Portuguese cemetery. Only two former members of the MWSO were present at her funeral – she had outlived most of them. Such was her remarkable tenacity.

♫

The Montreal Women's Symphony Orchestra was an essential contributor to the women's liberation movement. Its revolutionary work was so far ahead of its time that it is only now that its significance is beginning to be recognized and understood. Though they may not have considered themselves "feminists" at the time, the few MWSO members who are still alive speak of the orchestra as contributing to the crumbling of barriers for women in society at large and producing a new and confident generation of female musicians.

"Ethel didn't realize that she was really beginning a movement of feminism amongst women musicians...and neither did we," says Pearl Rosemarin Aronoff.

"You know, she didn't realize it, but she did it. She was a very strong-willed person...We started a movement...a movement of women in music," Lyse Vézina says proudly, and adds, "In those days, you had to fight your way in the world. I'm a fighter myself."

"We had to fight. We were women," echoes a violinist. "The orchestra was so far ahead of its time...so far ahead. Ethel was a visionary."

"The orchestra opened up many opportunities for women...it gave us confidence," emphasizes Violet Louise Grant States.

James P. Komar, a Montreal human rights activist, boasts that the MWSO "accomplished something never before done, and never again done, in any country. It was and remains something unique: something which has had a global impact." Arthur Kaptainis of the *Montreal Gazette* remarks that Ethel Stark and the MWSO helped to usher in a new era of "podium feminism."[75]

Ethel Stark also recognized the great importance and influence their work had in both the music world and society at large. In a letter to the *Montreal Gazette* in 1995, Ethel wrote:

> The Montreal Women's Symphony Orchestra discontinued its activities after 25 years due to a lack of funds, but what I set out to do was accomplished beyond my dreams. It must be remembered that women were unabashedly excluded from symphony orchestras. Today, a glance at any professional orchestra is enough to show how successful we were in gaining acceptance for women. We were a strong current in the rising tide that would sweep away the barriers to woman musicians, women in governments, industry and higher education.[76]

This women's movement in music served as a catalyst for social change that would shape society for generations to come. In shaking the foundations of the traditionally male symphony orchestra and by thrusting open the doors of equal opportunity to women of all walks of life, Ethel Stark and Madge Bowen also raised the status of women in society at large.

But the story of this ensemble of musical apprentices, the underdogs from Montreal who revolutionized music in Canada, is ultimately a story about the things that hold people of different nationalities, ethnicities, religions, social classes, and age together. It is about the power of music to transcend boundaries, to destroy prejudice, and to build up community. It is also a reminder that hard work and determination, sprinkled with a good dose of humor and generosity, can turn a dream into a reality.

AUTHOR'S NOTE

This book is a commemoration of the remarkable vision of two women, Ethel Stark and Madge Bowen, who imagined a place for regular working-class women – mothers, housewives, students, teachers, and office workers – on the orchestral stage. Despite formidable challenges, these women worked in harmony and embarked upon a remarkable journey that would help to change the status of women in the music profession in North America forever. Nonetheless, their stories are largely missing from historical records; their voices have remained almost completely silent.

Through years of research and travel, interviews and conversations with surviving MWSO members, their families, colleagues, and friends, I was able to piece together, little by little, an account of the MWSO as an organization. Their story fascinated and inspired me. And then one day, David Gutnick of the CBC stumbled upon the story and produced the radio documentary, "It Wasn't Tea Time: Ethel Stark and the Montreal Women's Symphony Orchestra" (2012). Sometime later the women from Second Story Press heard about it and were also captivated. Our common enthusiasm resulted in this book.

First, I express my sincerest gratitude to Max Haupt, Ethel

Stark's nephew, for his great generosity in sharing Dr. Stark's private papers, recordings, photographs, memorabilia, and unpublished memoir. Without his assistance, this book would not have been possible.

I also owe heartfelt gratitude to Lyse Vézina and Pearl Rosemarin Aronoff, two extraordinary musicians. Their candid accounts of their years in the women's orchestra – as well as their reflections on various issues – have been invaluable to my research.

My debt to Violet Grant States is also great, for sharing her personal account of her time in the orchestra as well as photographs and memorabilia. Mrs. Grant States has been an inspiration to me. I also wish to mention her sister and her niece, Joyce Grant Callender and Ivy Callender, for all their help in this project. Joyce, thank you for sharing your special highlights of the MWSO.

A heartfelt thanks to Susan Myers, Sonia Slatin's niece, who shared a lot of material about her beloved "Aunt Cyd," including private letters and photographs, and has remained enthusiastic about this project.

I also wish to mention the role of Madge Bowen's granddaughter, Ann Adair-Martin. I am grateful to her for all the time she devoted to sharing her recollections and photographs of her family. Without her assistance, this story would have been incomplete.

Thank you also to Denis Feldman, Nathalie Clair-Feldman's husband, for sharing his wife's story, as well as photographs. Thank you to part-time MWSO violinist Yaëla Hertz and concertmistress Mildred Goodman, for taking the time to share their thoughts and recollections of the orchestra and their friends and to Mary Terey-Smith and James P. Komar, Dr. Stark's secretary for many years.

Thanks to my dear professor, Friedemann Sallis, who first encouraged me to take on this project and has remained enthusiastic all these years.

Thank you to the ladies at the University of Calgary Library (Nancy, Sylvia, Cindy, and Marilyn), the staff at Library and Archives Canada (in particular Rachel Gagnon), the Jewish Public Library, and Bryan Martin at the University of Toronto Library.

I must also thank Margie Wolfe, Carolyn Jackson, Marianne

Ward, and the team at Second Story Press for their encouragement, support, and infinite patience, as well as David Gutnick of the CBC for his interest in my work.

Gratitude to my parents, brother, sister, and nephew, for their love and encouragement.

Most importantly, endless thanks to my best friend and husband, Kamil, for his loving support throughout, for his proofreading of the many drafts, for accompanying me throughout the country interviewing subjects, and for his frank comments.

Finally, to anyone else I may have missed, thank you.

FOOTNOTES

PROLOGUE

[1] Sanna Iitti, *The Feminine in German Song* (New York: Peter Lang, 2006), 34.

[2] Ibid., 35.

[3] Gustave Kerker, "Opinions of Some New York Leaders on Women as Orchestral Players," *Musical Standard* 21 (Apr. 2, 1904), 217–18.

[4] John Sherman, "Woman Harpist or Cellist is Top Sight at Concerts," *American String Teachers Association* 23, 2 (March–April 1962), 2.

[5] Quoted in Antoinette Handy, *Black Women in American Bands and Orchestras,* 2nd ed. (Lanham, MD: Scarecrow Press, 1998), 30.

[6] Beth Macleod, *Women Performing Music: The Emergence of American Women as Instrumentalists and Conductors* (Jefferson, NC: McFarland & Company, 2001), 15.

[7] Ibid.

[8] Ibid.

[9] Ethel Stark quoted in K. Linda Kivi, *Canadian Women Making Music* (Toronto: Green Dragon Press, 1992), 46.

CHAPTER 1

[10] Paul Helmer, *Growing With Canada: The Émigré Tradition in Canadian Music* (McGill-Queen's University Press, 2009), 86.

[11] Ethel Stark wrote her own memoir. Unfortunately, she passed away before she could publish it.

[12] Fritz Reiner quoted in Philip Hart, *Fritz Reiner: A Biography* (Evanston, IL: Northwestern University Press, 1997), 161.

CHAPTER 2

[13] Thomas Archer, "Notable Recital by Ethel Stark: Unusually Fine Playing Heard from Canadian Violinist Last Night," *Montreal Gazette*, November 30, 1933, 17. Thomas Archer became a fan of Ethel's early on and supported her with favorable reviews throughout her career. He considered her one of the best conductors in the country.

[14] Sondra Wieland Howe, *Women Music Educators in the United States: A History* (Lanham, MD: Scarecrow Press, 2014), 148.

[15] Linda Dempf, "The Woman's Symphony Orchestra of Chicago," *Notes – Quarterly Journal of the Music Library Association* (June 2006), 867.

[16] Some years after Ethel left, the orchestra also played music for movies and was featured in the 1945 film *Here Come the Co-Eds*.

CHAPTER 3

[17] "Women Musicians Urge Equal Rights: Opportunity for Jobs is Asked at Rally of New Organization Here," *New York Times*, May 19, 1938.

[18] "Women Yearn to Play Tuba and Bassoon," *New York Herald Tribune*, May 19, 1938.

CHAPTER 4

[19] Leslie Garden, "A Symphony of Women," *Chatelaine*, 1942. Library and Archives Canada, Ethel Stark fonds, Mus 242, 1993-19, Box 5, File 241/41.

[20] "Brief from the Montreal Women's Symphony to be presented to La Comission Royale des Problemes Constitutionnels." Library and Archives Canada, Ethel Stark Fonds, Mus 242-14, Box 242, June 28, 2011.

[21] Ethel Stark quoted in Olive Dickason, "Ethel Stark." Library and Archives Canada, Ethel Stark fonds, Mus 242.

[22] Some of the ensembles and musical organizations that already existed in 1940s Montreal were: The Société des concerts symphoniques de Montréal, the Montreal Orchestra, the McGill Chamber Orchestra, the Ladies' Morning Musical Club, the Montreal Festivals, the Opera Guild of Montreal (1941), and the Little Symphony of Montreal (1942), as well as various professional chamber music groups.

[23] Madge Bowen quoted in "Women in the War," *Montreal Herald*, January 3, 1942. Library and Archives Canada, Ethel Stark Fonds, Mus 242, 1993-19, Box 5, File 241/41.

[24] "A Women's Orchestra," *Fashion Magazine*, Montreal, (1946): 79.

[25] Ethel Stark quoted in Arthur Kaptainis, "Pioneer likes a challenge: Violinist and conductor Ethel Stark founded a women's symphony," *Montreal Gazette*, April 24, 2010.

[26] Esther Litman quoted in Albert Hunter, "History of Women's Symphony Recounts 10 Years Hard Struggle," *Montreal Gazette*, December 17, 1949, 23.

27 Alexander Brott and Betty Nygaard King, *My Lives in Music* (Montreal: Mosaic, 2005), 29–30. So displeased was the Goetzel family that their daughter had married a Jewish man that they sent her belongings to the marriage home in a cut up leather trunk on the day of her wedding. They would reconcile only years later.

28 Agathe de Vaux, *La Petite Histoire de l'Orchestra Symphonique de Montréal* (Montreal: Louise Courteau, 1984), 14.

29 Violet Archer, interview by Libby Smith, January 27, 1982. University of Alberta Archives, Violet Archer fonds, Box AV-8, Folder 33.

30 J.A. Thompson, "Music on a Shoestring," *New Liberty*, June 1950, 23.

CHAPTER 5
31 Ibid.

32 Hugh Thomson, "The Cold Toast of the Town," *Saturday Night*, August 6, 1960, 25.

33 Thomas Archer, "New Orchestra Prepares Debut," *Montreal Gazette*, July 4, 1940.

34 Ibid.

35 Dorothy W. Williams, "The Jackie Robinson Myth: Social Mobility and Race in Montreal, 1920–1960" (master's thesis, Concordia University, Montreal, 1999), 49.

36 The violinist was back to work with the orchestra three weeks after giving birth.

37 Howard Taubman, "An Even Break: Negro Instrumentalists Ask for a Chance to Earn Way into Ensemble," *New York Times*, April 22, 1956.

[38] H.P.B., "Ladies' Music Wins Success." Library and Archives Canada, Ethel Stark fonds, MUS 242, 1993-19, Box 3, File 33.

[39] Ibid.

[40] Ibid.

[41] Thomas Archer quoted in Frances Rooney, "The Montreal Women's Symphony," *Atlantis* 5, 1 (1979), 73.

CHAPTER 6
[42] Brenda Dalen, "The Composer's Voice: What Women Can Do," *Canadian University Music Review* 16, 1 (1995), 30.

[43] Ethel Stark quoted in "Quebec: Anniversary with Music," *Time*, March 6, 1950, 24.

[44] Ethel Stark, "Prelude: Thank you so much for your very kind words." Library and Archives Canada, Ethel Stark fonds, Mus 242, 19931-9, Box 1, File 242/1.

[45] Violet Archer quoted in Dalen, "The Composer's Voice," 31.

[46] Ibid., 17.

[47] Ibid., 30.

[48] "Women in the War," *Montreal Herald*, January 3, 1942.

[49] Mary Machim quoted in Ilse Zadrozny, "Stark Led Our First Female Orchestra," *Montreal Gazette*, November 4, 1995, C7. Mary also recalls that Ethel made "suspect players" perform their lines solo in front of the entire orchestra.

[50] Quoted in "Women in the War."

[51] There were several racially integrated "jazz" and "popular" groups and orchestras in the US before the 1950s, but I am not aware of

any "classical" full-fledged symphony orchestra in North America before the Second World War that engaged black musicians on a permanent basis.

[52] Unidentified publications. Library and Archives Canada, Ethel Stark fonds, MUS 242, 1993-19, Box 5.

CHAPTER 7

[53] Ethel Stark, "My Music Career…," Library and Archives Canada, Ethel Stark fonds, MUS 242-1, Box 1, June 28, 2011.

[54] Newspaper reports and MWSO member's accounts of how many women participated in the concert vary from 80 to almost 100.

[55] Irving Kolodin quoted in "Orchestra Built on $10 Bill and Love of Music," *Montreal Herald Tribune*. Library and Archives Canada, Ethel Stark fonds, Mus 242, 1993-19, Box 5.

CHAPTER 8

[56] Letter to Mr. Koudriavtzeff from Mr. Gorlinksky, November 10, 1947. Library and Archives Canada, Ethel Stark fonds, Mus 242, Box 3, File 29.

[57] Sonia Slatin, "Ethel Stark and the Montreal Women's Symphony Orchestra, Pioneers for Canada and Women" (paper presented at McGill University, Conference of Women's Union on Creative Women, March 12, 1975), 6. Mus 242, 1993-19, Box 3, Folder 30. Ethel Stark Fonds, Library and Archives Canada; and Thompson, "Music on a Shoestring," 23.

[58] Lyse Vézina, *Quarante ans au coeur de L'Orchestre symphonique de Montréal* (Quebec City: Varia, 2000), 31.

[59] Noriega, "The Emergence of Women as Professional Musicians," 50.

[60] Thomas Archer wrote, "She proved again that she is one of the most gifted conductors we have in the country." Thomas Archer,

"Ethel Stark Conducts," *Montreal Gazette*, December 18, 1959.

[61] The "Big Five" orchestras of the United States of America were: the New York Philharmonic, the Boston Symphony Orchestra, the Chicago Symphony Orchestra, the Philadelphia Orchestra, and the Cleveland Orchestra.

[62] Violet Archer, "Be sure, there are gentiles who care," *Montreal Star*, November 22, 1943. University of Alberta Archives, Violet Archer fonds, Box 89, file 5.

CHAPTER 9
[63] Slatin, "Ethel Stark," 11. Library and Archives Canada, Ethel Stark fonds, Mus 242, 1993-19, Box 3, Folder 30.

[64] Hugh Thomson, "Montreal Snubs Women's Symphony," *Toronto Daily Star*, March 7, 1959.

[65] Thomson, "Cold Toast of the Town," 25.

[66] Rooney, "The Montreal Women's Symphony," 76.

[67] Ibid.

[68] Archer quoted in Dalen, "Composer's Voice," 29–30.

[69] Stark, "To the 1960s." Library and Archives Canada, Ethel Stark fonds, MUS 242-1, Box 1, June 28, 2011.

CHAPTER 11
[70] The Société des concerts symphoniques de Montréal adopted the bilingual name Orchestre symphonique de Montréal/Montreal Symphony Orchestra in 1954.

[71] Violet Archer quoted in Dalen, 14.

[72] Violet Archer cited in Margaret Gillet and Ann Beer, *Our Own Agendas* (Ottawa: Carleton University Press, 1995), 80.

[73] Julie Ayer, *More Than Meets the Ear: How Symphony Musicians Made Labor History* (Minneapolis: Syren Book, 2005), 107.

[74] Letter from Ruth and Shepard Broad to Ethel Stark, August 30, 1979. Bay Harbour Island, Florida. Library and Archives Canada, Ethel Stark fonds, Mus 242.3. Box 1, June 28, 2011.

[75] Arthur Kaptainis, "Putting Down the Spatula Picking up the Baton," *Montreal Gazette*, March 9, 1991, H1/Break.

[76] Ethel Stark, "Woman Musicians Set the Pace for the Future," *Montreal Gazette*, November 19, 1995.

BIBLIOGRAPHY

Ammer, Christine. *Unsung: A History of Women in American Music*. Portland, Oregon: Amadeus Press, 2001.

Thomas Archer. "Ethel Stark Conducts." *Montreal Gazette*, December 18, 1959.

———. "Notable Recital by Ethel Stark: Unusually Fine Playing Heard from Canadian Violinist Last Night." *Montreal Gazette*, November 30, 1933.

Ayer, Julie. *More Than Meets the Ear: How Symphony Musicians Made Labor History*. Minneapolis: Syren Book, 2005.

Bowers, Jane and Judith Tick, eds. *Women Making Music: the Western Art Tradition, 1150–1950*. Urbana: University of Illinois Press, 1986.

Brott, Alexander and Betty Nygaard King. *My Lives in Music*. Montreal: Mosaic, 2005.

Dalen, Brenda. "The Composer's Voice: What Women Can Do." *Canadian University Music Review* 16, 1 (1995): 14–40.

Dempf, Linda. "The Woman's Symphony Orchestra of Chicago." *Notes, Quarterly Journal of the Music Library Association* (June 2006): 857–903.

De Vaux, Agathe. *La petite histoire de l'Orchestre symphonique de Montréal.* Montreal: Louise Courtae, 1984.

Downes, Olin. "Women's Symphony Makes Debut Here." *New York Times,* October 23, 1947.

Ethel Stark fonds. Mus 242. Library and Archives Canada.

Ethel Stark fonds. Montreal Jewish Public Library Archives.

Gillet, Margaret and Ann Beer. *Our Own Agendas: Autobiographical Essays by Women Associated with McGill University.* Ottawa: Carleton University Press, 1995.

Gutnick, David (producer). "It Wasn't Teatime: Ethel Stark and the Montreal Women's Symphony Orchestra." Radio documentary. Canadian Broadcasting Corporation, April 29, 2012.

Handy, D. Antoinette. *Black Women in American Bands & Orchestras,* 2nd ed. Lanham, MD: Scarecrow Press, 1998.

Hart, Philip. *Fritz Reiner: A Biography.* Evanston, IL: Northwestern University Press, 1997.

Helmer, Paul. *Growing with Canada: The Émigré Tradition in Canadian Music.* Montreal & Kingston: McGill-Queen's University Press, 2009.

Hinely, Mary Brown. "The Uphill Climb of Women in American Music: Performers and Teachers." *Music Educators Journal* 70, 8 (April 1984): 31–35.

Hout, Cécile and Maria L. Noriega. "Ethel Stark." *Encyclopedia of Music in Canada*, 2nd ed. Historica Foundation. http://www.thecanadianencyclopedia.com.

Hunter, Albert. "History of Women's Symphony Recounts 10 Years' Hard Struggle." *Montreal Gazette,* December 17, 1949.

Iitti, Sanna. *The Feminine in German Song*. New York: Peter Lang, 2006.

Jagow, Shelley M. "Women Orchestral Conductors in America: The Struggle for Acceptance—An Historical View from the Nineteenth Century to the Present." *College Music Symposium* 38 (1998): 126–45.

Kalbfleisch, John. "Pioneering Violinist, Conductor, Blazed Trail for Women." *Montreal Gazette*, February 2, 2003.

Kallmann, Helmutt. *A History of Music in Canada, 1534–1914*. Toronto: University of Toronto Press, 1960.

Kaptainis, Arthur. "Pioneer Likes a Challenge." *Montreal Gazette*, April 20, 2010.

———. "Putting Down the Spatula Picking up the Baton." *Montreal Gazette*, March 9, 1991, H1/Break.

Keillor, Elaine. *Music in Canada: Capturing Landscape and Diversity*. Montreal & Kingston: McGill-Queen's University Press, 2006.

Kerker, Gustave. "Opinions of Some New York Leaders on Women as Orchestral Players." *Musical Standard* 21 (April 2, 1904).

King, Joe. *From the Ghetto to the Main: The Story of Jews of Montreal*. Montreal: Montreal Jewish Publications Society, 2001.

Kivi, K. Linda. *Canadian Women Making Music*. Toronto: Green Dragon Press, 1992.

Legare, Celine. "La symphonie féminine se fait rare parce qu'elle est pauvre." *La Presse*, February 25, 1959.

Linteau, Paul-André. *Quebec Since 1930*. Halifax, NS: James Lorimer & Company, 1991.

MacDonald, Rose. "Montreal Women's Orchestra Here For Concert." *Toronto Evening Telegram*, April 12, 1946.

Macleod, Beth. *Women Performing Music: The Emergence of American Women as Instrumentalists and Conductors.* Jefferson, NC: McFarland & Company, 2001.

Noriega, Maria L. "The Montreal Women's Symphony Orchestra and the Emergence of Women as Professional Musicians (1940–1965)." Master's thesis, University of Calgary, 2010.

Rooney, Frances. "The Montreal Women's Symphony." *Atlantis* 5, 1 (1979): 70–81.

Schonberg, H.C. *The Great Conductors.* New York: Simon and Schuster, 1967.

Shattner, Sybil. "Letter to Editor: A Great Talent Remains 'Completely Neglected'." *Montreal Star*, September 6, 1975.

Sherman, John. "Woman Harpist or Cellist is Top Sight at Concerts." *American String Teachers Association* vol. 23, no. 2 (March-April 1962).

Slatin, Sonia and Maria L. Noriega. "The Montreal Women's Symphony Orchestra." *Encyclopedia of Music in Canada*, 2nd ed. Historica Foundation, 2012. http://www. thecanadianencyclopedia.com.

Stark, Ethel, Letter to the editor. "Woman Musicians Set the Pace for the Future." *Montreal Gazette*, November 19.

Taubman, Howard. "An Even Break: Negro Instrumentalists Ask for a Chance to Earn Way into Ensemble." *New York Times*, April 22, 1956.

Thompson, J.A. "Music on a Shoestring." *New Liberty*, June 1950, 22–23.

Thomson, Hugh. "Montreal Snubs Women's Symphony." *Toronto Daily Star*, March 7, 1959.

———. "The Cold Toast of the Town." *Saturday Night*, August 6, 1960: 25.

Vézina, Lyse. *Quarante ans au coeur de L'Orchestre symphonique De Montréal.* Quebec City: Varia, 2000.

Violet Archer fonds. University of Alberta Archives.

Wieland Howe, Sondra. *Women Music Educators in the United States: A History.* Lanham, MD: Scarecrow Press, 2014.

Williams, W. Dorothy. "The Jackie Robinson Myth: Social Mobility and Race in Montreal, 1920–1960." Master's thesis, Concordia University, Montreal, 1999.

"Women Musicians Urge Equal Rights: Opportunity for Jobs is Asked at Rally of New Organization Here." *New York Times*, May 19, 1938.

Zadrozny, Ilse. "Stark Led Our First Female Orchestra." *Montreal Gazette*, November 4, 1995.

PHOTO CREDITS

Canada, MUS 242, Box 5, Folder 41, 1993-19.

page 75: Courtesy of Violet Louise Grant States

page 80: Shutterstock

page 82: Courtesy Ethel Stark Estate

page 83: Courtesy Ethel Stark Estate

page 86: H.P.B., Ethel Stark Fond, Library and Archives Canada, Mus 242, 1993-19, Box 3, File 33.

page 88: The Montreal Daily Star, October 3, 1940, Photo by Notman, Ethel Stark Fond, Library and Archives Canada, Mus 242, 1993-19, Box 3, File 33.

page 91: LAC Ethel Stark Fond, Library and Archives Canada, Mus 242, 1993-19, Box 5, Folder 41, 1993-19.

page 92: Percy Grainger, Ethel Stark Fond, Library and Archives Canada, Mus 242/6, 1995-47.

page 93: Courtesy Violet Grant States

page 98: Weekend Magazine, Vol. 5, no. 6, 1955, Photos by Louis Jaques, Ethel Stark Fond, Library and Archives Canada, Mus 242, 1993-19.

page 103: Photo-Journal, Aug. 6, 1959, 33, Courtesy Violet Grant States.

page 107: Montreal Women's Symphony Orchestra, Conrad Poirier Fonds, Conrad Poirier, Bibliothèque et Archives nationales du Québec, item no. P48S1P12220.jpg.

page 114: Courtesy Violet Grant States

page 119: Ethel Stark Fond, Library and Archives Canada, Mus 242/6, 1995-47.

page 120: Courtesy Violet Grant States

page 122: Courtesy Ethel Stark Estate

page 123: La Presse, November 15, 1947, Ethel Stark Fond, Library and Archives Canada, Mus 242, 1993-19, Box 5, File 41.

page 124/125: Ethel Stark Fond, Library and Archives Canada, Mus 242/5, 1995-47.

page 129: From New Liberty magazine, courtesy Violet Grant States

page 134: Courtesy of Ann Adair-Martin

page 139: Courtesy Denis Feldman

page 141: Courtesy Violet Grant States

page 145: Canadian Music Centre

page 151: Courtesy of Lyse Vézina

page 169: Courtesy of David Gutnick

page 171: Ethel Stark Collection, Jewish Public Library Archives, Fonds no. 1255, item no. 006354.

page 172: Ethel Stark Estate

page 173: Clement Allard

ABOUT THE AUTHOR

MARIA NORIEGA RACHWAL is a music teacher and musicologist living in Toronto, Ontario. She has given many lectures on women in music throughout the country and written articles on the subject for professional organizations. Her work on the Montreal Women's Symphony Orchesta was featured on the CBC Radio documentary, "It Wasn't Tea Time: Ethel Stark and the Montreal Women's Symphony Orchestra."